Healing Your Life:
Recovery from Domestic Abuse

By

Candace A. Hennekens

PS & P

ProWriting Services and Press

© Copyright 1991, Candace A. Hennekens

All rights reserved. No part of this book may be reproduced in any form or by any electronic or mechanical means including information storage and retrieval systems without the prior written permission of the publisher, except by a reviewer, who may quote brief passages in a review. Published by ProWriting Services and Press, 415 Terrill Street, Chippewa Falls, Wisconsin 54729.

Printed in the United States of America.
First printing, soft cover.

ISBN 0-9630148-0-3

Library of Congress Catalog Card Number 91-90531.

10 9 8 7 6 5 4 3 2 1

Acknowledgements

Many persons deserve acknowledgement, but I would like to especially thank these individuals who played a key role in helping me emotionally during the hard work of producing this book. Those persons are: my mother, who listened to every detail of this venture with enthusiasm and interest; Kathie Butler who cheered me on especially in the days when I wasn't so sure this was a good idea; Judy Brown-Wescott who read my manuscript in various stages and gave me good suggestions; Karalyn Harrington who connected me with the idea of creating my own publishing company; Sandra Merwin who told me I could do it. I would also like to thank the guys down the hall who helped me with my computer, and my manager, Ray Thul, who recognized the importance of the project in my life. There are many others, but these were noteworthy in helping me follow the path to this book. I would also like to thank my daughters who always thought I should do this, no doubt about it. To all the other people who encouraged me to do this, I also give my thanks.

To all persons who reach out with love to others.

Table of Contents

	Bill of Rights for Survivors of Domestic Abuse	5
1	Purpose of This Book	6
2	My Story	10
3	Shame: The Enabler for Abuse	23
4	Feelings Are Guide Posts	33
5	Affirm Yourself	44
6	Career Planning Gives You Control	54
7	Goals: A Powerful Tool	69
8	You Can Build Healthy Relationships	80
9	You Are On the Path	93
	Bibliography	103

BILL OF RIGHTS

FOR

SURVIVORS OF DOMESTIC ABUSE

1. I will not be blamed or shamed for having been a victim.

2. I have the right to be happy.

3. I have the right to be free of all forms of abuse: physical, mental, emotional, psychological, or sexual.

4. I have the right to feel my feelings.

5. I have the right to take care of myself.

6 I have the right to have my needs met .

7. I have the right to make choices.

8. I have the right to be loved in a healthy way.

9. I have the right to live without fear.

10. I have the right to express myself.

11. I have the right to forgive myself for things in the past.

12. I have the right to make a better life for myself.

CHAPTER ONE

PURPOSE OF THIS BOOK

I have written this book for women who have left an abusive relationship. Drawing on my life's experiences, my reading of shame-based therapy books, drug and alcohol recovery literature, and my experience as a human resources practitioner, I have written a book for the woman who wants a better life. Although men are abused as well, statistics show that far fewer men are victims than women. I therefore have chosen to write as if I were speaking to women. I welcome male readers and hope the style does not distract from the content of the message.

If you are abused now, or are recovering from an abusive relationship, you can break the pattern. This book is about the steps that I took to do just that. I believe learning about them will help you do the same. I believe it is possible to change, to break former dysfunctional attitudes and behaviors and move on and become happy, whole human beings who reach their potential.

When I was twenty-two years old, I was like any other young woman -- full of life, expectations, excitement for life. I wrote an entry in my journal:

> My life is a kaleidoscope. Each day the scene is changed into another variety of an infinite set of events. Of course, I do not always think like this. I become disgusted and frustrated, frightened and yearn to run. But as I learned long ago, life will not hand us perfection. It is up to each person to make out of the best of life, the life of the best. I'm doing it in a fumbling, mistake-ridden way. I do not always do what I should, but I do my best, and always optimistically hope I may someday.

I am forty-two years old. I have been married twice, and both marriages were abusive relationships. The first marriage contained physical abuse; the second contained emotional abuse. I learned something from my first marriage and knew that physical violence was wrong, but I did not know enough to make the connection that physical abuse is only one form. In fact, in an abusive relationship, it is likely that several forms of abuse exist.

ABUSE DEFINED

I know now that abuse comes in many different forms. There is emotional abuse, putting the woman down or making her feel bad about herself, name-calling, telling her she's crazy, and playing mind games with her.

Physical abuse can be displayed as pushing, shoving, hitting, slapping, choking, pulling hair, punching, kicking, grabbing, twisting her arms, tripping, biting, beating, throwing the woman down, and using a weapon against her. In some cases, physical abuse goes as far as serious injury or death.

Purpose of book 9

There is sexual abuse, making her do sexual things against her will, and physically attacking the sexual parts of her body and treating her like a sex object.

Other techniques used to control the woman include isolating her so that the man controls what she does, who she sees and talks to and where she goes. Intimidation is also a power tool, putting her into a state of fear by using looks, actions, gestures, loud voices, smashing things, and destroying property.

Economic abuse is another control tool, including trying to prevent the woman from getting or keeping a job, making her ask for money, giving her an allowance, or taking money away from the woman.

Men also use the power of threats, making and/or carrying out threats to do something to hurt her emotionally. The man may threaten to take the children away, commit suicide, or report her to authorities.

Men can also use male privilege, treating her like a servant, making all the big decisions and acting like the master of the castle. This is also a form of abuse.

All these forms of abuse involve the man maintaining power and control over the woman. The continuum of abuse varies with each situation; the abuse might include elements of all the types, or just one type. The severity might vary. The bottom line is that none of these abusive behaviors is acceptable. Mild or severe, you have the right to better treatment.

After my second divorce, I was determined to break the pattern that had created so much pain for me. I began counselling, and over a period of years worked on developing a love for myself to attain higher self-esteem. It was only when I had made significant progress in this area that I realized why it had been so hard to break the pattern, the cycle of abuse. I had married my first husband at the age of 22. When we divorced, I was 31. Those nine years accounted for about one-third of my life. Starting a second marriage almost immediately after my first marriage and staying in that marriage six years accounted for another fifteen percent. By the time I had left that marriage, forty percent of my life and eighty percent of my adult life had been spent interacting with a husband in a dysfunctional way. No wonder the years I have spent free of dysfunctional intimate relationships seem like "baby steps." They account for only ten percent of my life. To be free of those patterns has taken tremendous work and conscious effort.

I have learned a lot about self-esteem: what it is, how it feels, how to nurture it in yourself and others. Those changes and my learnings are what I have to share with you. The journey I have taken over these twenty years has been painful, and hard. But I have learned and my life is at last a happy fulfilling life. You too have it in your power to shape the life you want. This book is for you to gain some ideas on how to do that. It is not the only way, but it is the way I did it.

This saying appeared in a church newsletter. I think it is appropriate to you:

"There are no paths in life except the ones we make by walking on them."

CHAPTER TWO

MY STORY

I will begin my story with Mother's Day, 1978. It was on that day that my husband chose to batter and beat me viciously. He didn't give me a Mother's Day present. I cried to him that he should have remembered. He vented his anger by attacking me after I had gone to bed. He came into the bedroom where I was sleeping, and woke me by sitting on my chest, putting his hands around my throat, and squeezing while repeating over and over, "I could kill you. I could kill you."

The fear I felt then is still real to me. I knew he could kill me at that moment, and thought he would. I fought back. I pushed, and kicked, and got him off. I ran into the kitchen to call the police. He chased after me and grabbed me, throwing me across the room. I tried again. He threw me again, then pushed me down and beat me across the back with his fists, then kicked and then beat again. Sobbing and crying, I thought I was going to get killed. I ran again, back to the bedroom, and he beat on me some more.

Then suddenly, he stopped, left the room, and left me alone. Through pounding ears, I heard my little girl's crying and knew we had awakened her. I went to the bathroom and washed my face in cold water, then looked up to the mirror and saw myself. My neck was covered with red welts, bruises were starting to form. I uncovered my back and saw more red marks. I was shaking and breathing hard.

I know I went into my daughter's room to comfort her. She was burning up with fever and I took her temperature, then gave her some Tylenol and got her to go back to sleep. But I felt numb; I knew I had barely escaped and I was stunned by the severity of the abuse. He had hit me before. He had punched me, threatened me with a knife, dragged me down the hall by my hair when I was pregnant, kicked me in the stomach, twisted my arm behind my back, hit me in the face, hit my ear so hard it swelled up like a boxer's, and thrown things at me. But he had never strangled me and he had never said he would kill me. He had called me "crazy", "a bitch", and other foul names. He had blamed me for every problem he ever had. He had diminished my every accomplishment and he had belittled me.

But this time the fury was stronger than I had ever felt. I felt his savagery in his body, and saw it in his face. I knew I had to do something, but I didn't know what.

I lay on the bed in the spare room, empty and afraid, until morning. I heard him get up, get dressed, and prayed he'd leave me alone. He left for work as usual, and I then got up, got up my daughter, and made an appointment to take her to see her pediatrician later on that day. I sat around in my pajamas listlessly until late morning, realizing I was in a state of shock, but unsure of what to do. I remembered that the city where I was living had just had a refuge house for battered wives open. I tried to find it in the phone book, but could not. It never occurred to me to call the police, directory assistance, or any source of help. I felt completely alone. As the day wore on, I started to panic and I called a good friend; she wasn't home. I called a neighbor; she wasn't home. I sat around some more. Finally I got dressed, wearing a turtleneck to cover my bruises. My eyes were red, puffy, and bloodshot from crying. I looked awful, and felt awful.

By mid-afternoon, my husband had not called to apologize and the thought of his return at dinner time scared me. It scared me into action. As a last resort, I called my sister in Wisconsin. I only spoke her name, but she knew immediately I was not okay. When I told her what had happened she said, "Pack your clothes and come home. I will call Mother and tell her you're coming. Go to Mother's. You'll be safe there. We'll decide what you should do later." I did as she told, and in an hour had thrown most of my daughter's and my clothes into the back seat of my car in a big pile. I added toys, a few other personal items, and took off for the doctor.

At the pediatrician's office, the doctor studied me carefully. He finally asked if I was okay, but I assured him that I was. Finally he turned his attention to my daughter. She had an ear infection so he prescribed an antibiotic, and I needed to go to the pharmacy to pick it up before I could leave. Realizing I had not packed any food, and had very little money and that we would be on the road until late that night, I drove back home and went into the kitchen to prepare my daughter's bottles and make some sandwiches.

Just as I was finishing, the phone rang. It was my husband and his voice was syrupy sweet. "I'm so sorry about last night."

I waited for a minute, but he had stopped talking. I said, "It's too late. I've had enough. I'm leaving."

He sputtered in indignation. "Leaving? You can't leave. You deserved what I gave you."

I slammed the receiver down, grabbed my daughter, and ran to the car. I was on the road and driving when I realized I had finally done it; I had left him. I had ended the misery I had been living with for years.

A counsellor once said to me that the hardest part is to leave. The trauma that follows isn't easy, but the hardest thing is to leave. I'd have to agree. Although I had often fantasized that I was free and happy during that marriage, I never thought I would really pack my bags and go. The fear that I really was a "bitch", that "I made him do it" always stopped me. I was not "the type" who divorced. I believed everyday that "things would get better." I had no self-esteem and most of my confidence had been eroded by living with a man who acted like a tyrant whenever I crossed him.

LIVING WITH FEAR BECOMES NORMAL

Living in fear became normal after a while. I forgot that there was any other way to live. I watched other couples relate on an equal basis and felt envy, but then the thought that their relationship might be as sick as my husband's and mine crossed my mind. I had learned you couldn't trust appearances. For we seemed, I am sure, to be a perfectly happy couple, raising a beautiful daughter, and enjoying life. My husband was a college professor. I had worked off and on, and was now staying home to raise our family. We owned a lovely home in a nice neighborhood. We travelled, collected antiques, and were involved in the community. Sometimes, in fact, we were happy, but more and more, the abuse reared its head when I least expected it, and I always had to have my guard up in fear. So instead of leaving, I fantasized about my husband's death, in a car accident, plane accident, some type of accident. But that day, I had somehow gotten up the courage to leave on my own.

When I left that day in 1978, I had some awareness that this was not a normal way of life and I truly wanted to be happy. But I didn't know what happiness was. I had kept the abuse a secret from family and friends. The only time I had sought intervention was when my husband attacked me while I held my daughter in my arms. That time I called the police. They came quickly and my husband was scared away. I told him at the time that I would leave if he ever touched me again. I didn't know if I really meant it, but it kept him in line for a year.

The divorce went fairly smoothly. Custody of our daughter was never an issue. We argued over money. In the end, I received a monetary settlement which was enough to get me back on my feet even though it did not represent an equitable division of property. I had also found a good job as editor of a company newspaper which drew upon my college training in journalism and previous editing experience. But I was frightened and felt alone. At 31, life seemed bewildering, and lonely.

I did some therapy and introspection work while I was getting divorced. I joined a support group for abused women and gained some insight and support. This was over ten years ago and spousal abuse was just beginning to get the public's attention. I was surprised at the common threads between us. Most women feel they are the cause of abuse and tend to keep the abuse a secret if they can. Most husbands blame their wives for the violence. I learned that abuse happens to all types of people -- rich and poor, young and old, educated or not. There is no typical abuser nor abused spouse. While alcohol is often involved, it doesn't have to be present. It was obvious to me that it happens often. It wasn't just my secret; many woman share the same secret.

Even though the support group was helpful, I was still a very needy person, needy for love and hungry for approval that I was okay. I was needy for being needed. I met a man who was as needy as I. We got along fine. He immediately swept me up in a whirlwind romance. We danced, fished, camped, listened to music, and had fun together. He excited me emotionally and I felt alive for the first time in years. I believe I truly loved him despite the superficiality of our relationship.He begged me to move in with him, which I did, bringing my daughter. Once there, the next step was marriage, and I gave him part of my divorce settlement to pay off his old bills. It looked like we were making a new beginning together.

Meanwhile my job required that I operate without much supervision and I figured out how to do the things I was responsible for. The job challenged me. I began to see how capable I really was. The company promoted me and I thought to myself, "Hey! This is fun!" I was having a good time. I needed my husband a little less because I had more going on in other areas of my life.

About two years after our marriage, I had another daughter. She was as beautiful as my first daughter, and my capacity to love increased. I began to understand that there is an unending supply of love in human beings. I needed a little less from my husband, but wanted more.

SHIFT FROM NEEDING TO WANTING

The shift from needing to wanting is a shift from weakness to strength. Needing to love someone and wanting to love someone are quite different. When you need someone, the more dependent they are, the better you feel because you are threatened by any changes in their perception of personal power. My husband felt threatened by my growing sense of personal power. He didn't want me to grow or change. He feared I would grow away from him.I wanted him to grow with me. I wanted more intimacy. I wanted communication, appreciation and closeness between us. He responded by becoming rigid. He wanted me to want only what he wanted, and if I didn't, he denigrated those goals as worthless, silly, and crazy.

The power struggle between us lasted four years. I continued to grow and he reacted with rigidity. When that failed, he attacked me indirectly through my daughter from my first marriage. He was verbally abusive to her. He would call her names. He would criticize her without end. He sometimes physically put himself between her and me; he apparently was so jealous of my affection for her that he could not bear to let us be together. Their relationship worried me greatly and began to dominate our life. I begged him to be kind. I took him to counselling. I prayed. Even my mother tried to help by coming to stay at the house when I travelled on business. I actually left him for two short periods of time. The first time I rented an apartment. The second time I stayed with my mother. But both times I went back because he promised to change. However, after our daughter's birth, the abuse increased and he would not admit that he had a problem feeling jealous of my daughter. The more I persisted in my demands that he treat her with respect, the more he persisted in his abuse.

To make a long story short, I finally left him for good, taking both girls because I knew he could not change, and if I wanted something better for myself and for my daughters, I would have to end the marriage. I asked myself the old Ann Landers' question, "Would my life be better off with him or without him?" I felt he was a poor parent, and I was concerned he would damage these beautiful children with his constant criticism and abuse, the result of his immaturity. If I died, unexpectedly, I didn't want him raising my daughters. That is a strong statement to make about the father of your child and your husband.

Again, the hardest part was to leave. I had desperately wanted a happy marriage. That had always been my strongest desire. Now as a once-divorced woman, about to be twice-divorced, I felt ashamed of

18   My story

those failed marriages. Before I left, I mentally gave him a year to change, but when I saw that he would not because he saw no reason to change, I decided my life would be better off without him. I left.

Life was terrible when I left. I had no real plans in place past the leaving. But once gone for what I said was for good, he reacted viciously and showed no mercy towards me. I truly thought my life was over. I felt immeasurable shame that I was getting divorced. I was stressed by the changes the separation created. I had moved out, leaving most of my possessions and household belongings behind. I literally had to start all over again. I didn't know what to do or how to carry on. My family and friends told me that I had done the right thing and life would improve, but I didn't believe them. I moved in with my mother for a few months, but I needed a place of my own so I bought a modest home with the rest of my divorce settlement from my previous marriage. I was afraid I might go back but each step of permanence away from him made it less likely.

That period is essentially a blank period for me. I have no memory of how I acted, or what I did during that time. My mother tells me that I was constantly doing things, never sitting down. How I continued to perform on my job is a mystery to me. I actually got promoted to a new position during that time frame, further adding to my stress. Not only did I move my residence but now my office and job were changed. The only things that remained the same for me were my car and my clothes. Sometimes when I drove to work or back home, I would get confused and panic, unable to remember where I was supposed to go.

It took the shock of discovering that my second husband had been married four times previously, and had several children from those marriages, to end my state of numbness. I was under the impression that he had been married twice, and had a daughter who was twenty. His daughter had lived with us for a time but had used drugs, stolen from me, and created a great deal of trouble and had been put in jail. The only reason I learned of his past was because my attorney was a criminal and divorce attorney who had suspicions about my husband's hostile actions towards me. The attorney had said he had a hunch there was something in his past he was hiding from me. He asked for permission to investigate. I remember laughing at him, saying he wouldn't find anything, but go ahead and investigate. He uncovered the divorce records and sent me copies. I was dumbfounded.

Obviously, my second husband had deliberately withheld the truth to manipulate me into marriage. I saw that he had wanted a family, a hardworking wife with some money, and when I no longer cooperated with his private plan, he retaliated. My attorney would not let me confront my husband. The facts would be used in the custody dispute.

The discovery of those lies caused immense pain, and I thought I would die. The dishonesty from someone who supposedly loved me hurt me deeply and I thought of it constantly. I asked over and over, "How could he have deceived me so?

BEGINNING AGAIN

During that black period, I spent several months reviewing every piece of paper from my past life. I reread all my journals. I looked at all the old photo albums. I went through all my boxes of memorabilia, old letters, and knickknacks. At the end of the review of my life, I had a better picture of myself: an intelligent woman who had never had a lot of self-esteem and confidence, who had wanted very much to please others and who had gotten hooked into first one relationship that was dysfunctional and then because the pattern was there and the needs were real, into another. Under the history of abuse, there still was a woman who was strong emotionally, and had a lot of things going for her: a good mother of two beautiful daughters, professionally successful, physically healthy and attractive, and willing to work hard. Could I begin again? The answer didn't come over night.

I struggled for months, fighting bitterness, anger, self-pity. My misery was worsened by the child custody dispute my husband and I were fighting. He had threatened when I left that he "would put me through hell" and that's what he was doing. The thought of losing my daughter to him tortured me. Despite assurance from my attorney that this would not happen, I spent many nights lying in bed worrying, unable to sleep.

But the other choice -- to become bitter, angry, and closed off from the joy of living and people was repugnant to me. I have always been open and trusting with the world. I felt it was a core part of my personality. I had had enough going on even in the abusive, hard times, to see that life could be rewarding, exciting, and fun. I needed people to live fully, and I have respect, compassion, and trust for most people. I had become friends with a woman who was also going through a divorce and she was bitter and angry. Her poison frightened me. Did I want to be like that? I knew there would always be ups and downs, but at 38, I had not even lived half of my life and I wanted to try. To quote the old saying, "When life hands you a lemon, make lemonade." I felt I had been cheated out of happiness, but I wanted to try to find happiness in the second half of my life. I didn't believe it was too late, but I wasn't sure it was in my power. One morning while drinking my coffee and thinking of another joyless day ahead, I vowed to myself that I would start fresh. I knew if I did not, my ex-husbands would dominate me for the rest of my life, even though we were no longer married.

INITIAL EFFORTS

My initial efforts to make a better life were simple. I decided to pursue the goal of an advanced degree. Because of the child custody dispute, I knew the divorce was going to last another year, and I thought I might as well begin to make progress on a positive goal. I thought a positive goal would pull me forward to the present and the future. I enrolled in a compressed two-year graduate program in management science. My employer picked up the tuition costs, making it financially feasible. My mother offered to come to my home and care for my children while I went to class. She made supper, and took my daughters to their ballet lessons. By this time, I was a manager of personnel for the same company I had started with eight years ago. The company was growing rapidly and it was a very exciting place to work. Between school, work, kids, improving and maintaining the house I had bought, I had every minute of my life occupied with activities and responsibilities. There was more to do than I could accomplish. Soon I was so busy that replaying history and lamenting the past happened less and less. I was so focused on the present and getting everything done that I didn't have time to focus on the past.

Twelve months later when my divorce went through and I received custody of my second daughter, the activities of school and work again kept me focused. By now I was working on my thesis and I was determined to finish the program after the hundreds of hours I had put into my degree. The divorce, which truly brought the ending I had wanted, also dredged up unhappy and uncomfortable emotions. As much as I wanted it, it was a real ending. Despite the dishonesty and difficult divorce, I still remembered the loving times and felt sadness that the marriage was over.

My story

I was facing life alone, with two young children to support and raise. The future was frightening. Yet, at the same time, I felt excitement. I felt like I had a clean slate and could form the life I wanted. I was beginning to heal, and could see that life would get better if I let it. School was keeping me focused on that beginning and gave me a sense of purpose. On July 4, 1987, one day after I was divorced, I woke up ready to test this new woman. Here is the rest of the story and how I did it--and am doing it today.

RECOMMENDATIONS FOR FURTHER WORK

If you're still in an abusive relationship, take steps to be safe:

1. Tell family and friends about the abuse. Keeping it a secret only maintains the power and control over you. Ask for their help.

2. Police departments exist to protect you. If you need to, call them. They will come to your aid. Some states now require the abuser to be arrested if the abuse occurs several times.

3. A safe house for abused women may exist in your community. Call them for more information. Flee if you have to. Their resources will keep you safe while you consider your options.

4. Ask yourself, "Would I be better off with him or without him?" If the answer is with him, get counselling for both of you. If he won't go, go alone.

If you've left an abusive relationship:

1. Know your legal rights. See a competent lawyer. Get a restraining order if you think you need to protect yourself from further violence or harassment.

2. Recognize that you are a person who is hurting. Take advantage of the counselling available at safe houses.

CHAPTER THREE

SHAME: THE ENABLER FOR ABUSE

When I began therapy as part of my healing, my counselor and I talked a lot about shame. I define shame as that deep-down feeling that you are worthless; you're not good enough at anything you do. You're not appropriate to life. The feeling of not being appropriate is all inclusive, what you do or say, how you act, dress or look. Nothing is right. You feel like a masquerader and even you don't know what's under the mask. Hearing about the feeling I'd had for so long and having it defined as shame was a life-changing experience. For me, it was like being born for a second time.

Shame had made me feel worthless, lacking in most things and inappropriate to life and yet others saw me as confident and competent. Shame had bound me in dysfunctional relationships to men. Shame was a jailer that kept me locked away from reaching my potential. The more I read and learned about shame, the more I was convinced that it was an illness and because it was an illness, there was a way to cure it. I decided to take shame on, so to speak, and rid it from myself and just that knowledge and will -- that I had it, that I could cure it, that I wanted to cure it -- was enough to begin to set me free to build a better life.

Shortly after I began counselling, I had a truly extraordinary experience, one that I have told few about for fear that they would think I was crazy. One night as I got into bed and lay my head on the pillow, I heard a whisper. I sat bolt upright and said, "What?" Silence. The next night the same thing happened. I sat upright and said, "What?" This time a voice from inside my head said, "I love you." I was dumbfounded. "What?" I asked again. The voice answered again, "I love you." That was it.

I believe my therapy had awakened my inner self, and as I struggled with my sense of worthlessness and despondency over my situation, my inner self rallied to my cause -- its cause -- to show support. The voice never returned. Nonetheless it was a real experience.

I am also convinced that though I understand shame from a theoretical base, from a therapeutic base, and from a life experience base, I will always be fighting shame. It is not like riding a bicycle, once you learn you never forget how. Shame needs to be slain everyday, in many ways. It is a life-long battle once you've had it dominate your life. Today I use affirmations. I deal with my feeling. I have positive relationships. I nurture myself. My bedside table contains shame-based therapy books that I read every day. For me, the message bears repeating over and over. I am worthy just as I am for who I am. Maybe someday I'll win the battle. Maybe someday I'll believe that everyday, all day for an endless number of days. I'll keep fighting shame as long as I have to because shame is insidious, and spreads once the seed has been planted.

I have read a lot on shame. Books by Merle Fossum and Marilyn Mason, Gershen Kaufman, Melody Beattie and John Bradshaw have been the cornerstones of my recovery. Even if you have never read a book or article on shame, there is no doubt in my mind that you are really the resident expert on shame. You know shame inside and out. You know how it feels, and how it poisons your life. You know that it is an enabler to get you to buy into a sick relationship and stay with it. What you don't know is how to get rid of it. Someday, if you keep trying, you'll know those things and will apply them to your life.

THE DEFINITION OF SHAME

Merle A. Fossum and Marilyn Mason in their book Facing Shame, Families in Recovery, define shame as "an inner sense of being completely diminished as a person. It is the self judging the self.....A pervasive sense of shame is the ongoing premise that one is fundamentally bad, inadequate, defective, unworthy, or not fully valid as a human being."

The authors differentiate shame from guilt. "Guilt is the developmentally more mature, though painful, feeling of regret one has about behavior that has violated a personal value."

They also say, "While guilt is a painful feeling of regret and responsibility for one's actions, shame is a painful feeling about oneself as a person."

They define a shame-bound family as a "group of people, all of whom feel alone together." Shame is masked in different family systems. There is the fairy tale family, which is too good to be true, where a game is played and roles are assumed. Family members deny their pain and keep their masks on to hide from the truth. The fairy tale family is often envied because it looks so good from the outside. Another family mask is the disconnected family, where family members move away from each other and their rituals. Closeness has been abandoned and family members lose touch with each other. Often great geographical distance is put between family members, and important dates and names are forgotten and not celebrated. In the rough and tough family, the mask is highly defined gender roles. Macho men and passive women push intimacy away by never being vulnerable and blame is laid on someone else. The belief is that life is hard. Finally, the nice-nice family mask covers up bad things. Interaction is characterized by smiles. Conflict is avoided and covert manipulation is used to manipulate family members.

PATTERNS OF DYSFUNCTIONAL FAMILIES

In a shame-bound family, which I call dysfunctional in other parts of my book, there are patterns to the way people interact. There are three patterns identified by Fossum and Mason from their work with clients. The patterns are on a continuum. Most families fall somewhere within the continuum. They distinguish between shamebound and respectful systems in three ways:

1. Violation of person versus violation of values.
2. Self with vague boundaries versus self as separate and part of a larger system.
3. Perfectionism versus accountability.

The first pattern, violation of the person rather than violation of values, means when a woman is abused, the family system she is in tells her she is bad, a bitch, unworthy, and other negative messages. As part of the dysfunctional system, she accepts this premise rather than the premise that it is wrong to be abusive to your partner when anger or emotions control you.

In the second pattern, self as separate and part of a larger system versus vague boundaries, the boundary between where you end and the family system begins has never been clearly defined. Instead of give and take and each having a place, the abuser may see the spouse as someone to serve his needs alone. When needs collide, the message is sent that you are wrong not to share those needs or see things that way.

In the third pattern, accountability versus perfectionism, persons are held accountable by being told that the person who has made a mistake is defective. It's the opposite of love the person not the behavior; it's love the behavior, hate the person. If the behavior is wrong, hate the person. This is the most damaging aspect of shame-bound systems. Psychological abuse springs from this pattern.

RULES OF BEHAVIOR IN SHAME-BOUND SYSTEMS

There are rules of behavior that flow from shame-bound systems. One rule is to be in control of all behavior and interactions. Here you see the abuser controlling others by the use of violence, intimidation and fear. Many women keep the violence secret out of shame which allows it to continue to exist as a control tool. Domestic argument laws and safe houses are societal tools which defuse violence as the controller. The woman has alternatives to call the police or leave the home.

There is the rule of perfectionism, the belief that you must always be right and always do the right thing. The perfectionism rule does not acknowledge that we are human and as human beings are bound to make mistakes. There is no forgiveness for mistakes and they may be constantly brought up.

Another rule is to blame someone if something doesn't go right. The blame can be laid on yourself or others. For women in an abusive relationship, the blame is frequently laid on them by their mates. If they were such and such a way, their husbands wouldn't beat them. If they did such and such a thing, their husbands wouldn't abuse them. This pattern is used by the abuser to maintain the image to himself of being in control. By blaming the partner, he rids himself of responsibility.

Another rule is denial. Deny feelings, especially the negative or vulnerable ones like anxiety, fear, loneliness, grief, rejection, and need.

The next rule concerns unreliability. Don't expect reliability or constancy in relationships. Watch for the unpredictable. Any woman in an abusive relationship knows that she can never know what might happen next. One minute things are going fine at home; the next minute her husband is throwing her across the room because of some transgression on her part. Abused women become certain that happiness is transitory at best.

Another rule concerns resolution of differences. In a shame-bound system there is incompleteness. Transactions aren't completed or resolved. Poor communication occurs after the abuse so it cannot be addressed or corrected. When I was being physically abused, my husband never made reference to any of the incidents once they were over. It was as if, in his mind, they had never occurred. This incompleteness haunted me for years. It took me ten years to close the door on it.

Finally, there is no talk in shame-bound systems. Don't talk openly and directly about the shameful, abusive, or compulsive behavior. Disqualify it, deny it, or disguise it. For a woman who is not feeling anything, this is easy to do. The actions of her abusive partner are rationalized away. This keeps the incompleteness incomplete so to speak.

EFFECTS OF PATTERNS AND RULES

The patterns and rules of shame-based interactions have had a cumulative erosive action on your beliefs about yourself. Shaming interactions don't nurture your beliefs that you are a unique and precious individual worthy of love and respect just because you're you. The shaming interactions, especially because they have come from someone you allowed to be close to you and felt intimate with have been much more damaging than if they came from casual friends or daily contacts.

Over and over, your abuser had told you that you are bad. If an event outside of your control occurred, blame was laid, perhaps on you. You were not only blamed, you were told you were bad. You were told that to be lovable, you had to be perfect. No mistakes were allowed. There was no respect for who you were. If you didn't like something or want to do something, your desires or preferences were often not taken into account. Your husband, unable to acknowledge feelings, denied not only his but yours as well. They were labelled, if expressed by you, as crazy or absurd, or ignored. When you argued with your husband, the argument never ended. It just went underground until it reappeared in another form, same issue, different circumstances.

All these crazy rules drove you crazy, drove you to doubting yourself, your sanity, your perceptions of yourself, your feelings, your thoughts, your competence as a person. You have come away from the experience as a walking but wounded person. You have to learn techniques which will restore that fundamental belief in self that is vital to living a productive and satisfying life.

I am not addressing the issue of whether the abused or abuser brought these shame-based patterns into the relationship. Perhaps they were brought in by one or both of the parties. Perhaps the abused only wanted to please her spouse and bought into the system unconsciously. I believe even healthy individuals exposed to shame-based patterns and rules will take them on and internalize them after literally hundreds of thousands of exposures to the same message. Even the strongest human spirit can be beaten down by constant exposure. The question of why you were so vulnerable is an academic one. It is worthy of some work on your part to uncover your answer. However, the real payoff comes from recognizing that you are shame-bound and learning how to unbind from it. Shame is passed on. If you break your chain, you can break the chain for your children.

Immediately after leaving my first marriage, I asked myself over and over, "Why didn't I leave earlier?" The frequency of my question was almost self-torture. I blamed myself, over and over, for staying. Years later, I am able to stand back and see that the question was prompted by the old monster shame. The question was the quintessence of the self judging the self. I was not the one who used violence, force, and intimidation to get my way in the relationship. My fault was merely to submit out of a desire to keep a relationship intact.

I recall the first incidence of violence in my first marriage when I bought into the rules of conduct. We had gone on a delayed honeymoon, two months after our marriage, to the East Coast. We were staying in an idyllic bed and breakfast in the seaside town of Mystic, Connecticut. I was in love with my husband. He had gone out fishing on a chartered fishing vessel and came back excited and thrilled about catching several large blue fish. I, on the other hand, had spent the day finding things to do in the town, a little lonely and shy. That night when we were in bed, I crawled closer to him to cuddle after he had fallen asleep. Instead of returning the gesture with affection, or even just patting me on the behind with love, he woke up and shoved me hard onto the floor, then said, "Don't you ever get on my side of the bed again." I was 22 years old, staying in a strange hotel surrounded by strangers. I stifled my crying and lay there most of the night, my heart broken. The cycle of shame had begun, and I had blamed myself for not being more sensitive.

TRANSFORMING SHAME

Chinese philosophy talks about embracing your enemy. Just as the willow tree bends with the wind, our spirits can embrace shame and bend with it to transform it into part of our self. But instead of the self judging the self, shame embraced becomes only a piece of ourself. It takes its place with the nurturing part, with the joyful part, the sexual part, the serious part, the coaching part, the curious part, etc. and becomes just another piece. Shame in healthy proportion can help us be an analyzer that sees experiences and problems from a different viewpoint. It can help us analyze problems from a fuller perspective so that all courses of actions are considered. It teaches us to learn from our mistakes.

Shame needs to be cut down to size so that it is just one part of us, balanced by the many other parts, not the only viewpoint we have towards ourself. Antidotes to shame-bound behavior at first need to be constantly practiced until you've learned new habits. It will take time to counter the many messages you have received. Handle your human behavior gently. Don't blame yourself for every problem and mistake. Tune in to your feelings, knowing you are not going to act on every one. Talk about your feelings and trust that they are valid. Own them. Understand that happiness can be your continuum rather than unhappiness. Problems occur but every problem has a solution. Be less ready to create a crisis when none exist.

The irony of life is that though the thread that ties us to life is very fragile, the spirit to live is strong. You have the will, the drive to overcome your obstacles and to triumph over bad. The rest of this book is dedicated to specific techniques to bring shame and your recovery from it into proper perspective.

RECOMMENDATIONS FOR FURTHER WORK

1. By understanding that you have been shamed, you can begin the journey back to a healthy attitude about yourself. Read some of the books on shame. I recommend:

Codependent No More, by Melody Beattie, 1987, Harper/Hazelden Publishers.

Beyond Codependency, by Melody Beattie, 1989, Harper/Hazelden Publishers.

Men Who Hate Women and the Women Who Love Them, by Susan Forward and Joan Torres, 1986, Bantam Books.

Healing the Shame that Binds You, by John Bradshaw, 1988, Health Communications, Inc.

There is much literature in the alcohol and drug recovery field. Avail yourself of it; most of it applies.

2. Share your story and listen to the story of other women. The common threads will help you come to terms with your shame.

CHAPTER FOUR

FEELINGS ARE GUIDE POSTS

This is an entry from my journal. I wrote it shortly after I had left my second marriage. The symbolism of being safe in a box illustrates what happens to the feelings of a woman trapped in an abusive relationship:

> She could feel the box form around her. To keep his meanness from coming in to her, she slowly shut the doors around her. The price for doing this was great. The emptiness within her was bigger and hurtful, but she protected herself. Her spirit had always co-existed with emptiness. It could handle the disappointment. His threat was too great to let him in. He would destroy her if his barbs and twisted distortions came inside always. So slowly, door by door, she shut him out. The doors were heavy, hinged with golden clasps. The

wood was shiny from varnish and shone golden like wheat fields decked with sun. The doors came around her spirit like a circle with angles, an octagon guarding her, protecting her...The doors came to have locks. First only at the bottom, then at the middle and finally at the top. The golden locks were beautiful. Delicate yet sturdy, they were handcrafted and shone warmly against the wood.

One day, she could stand it no longer. She took all the keys, put them in a midnight blue velvet drawstring bag, and threw the keys into her emptiness.

The bag whirled around and around and around and then disappeared.

She looked around at her walls. There was so much emptiness here. Yet , in a corner was a warm little spot and she knew she was safe and warm, even in the emptiness.

In order to survive, I learned not to feel. My husband would reject my feelings and to legitimize that rejection, I rejected them as well. Over a period of years, feelings of closeness, joy, enthusiasm, sadness, happiness, frustration, anger, and love were chunked off and frozen. Eventually all I had left was a chronic state of depression due to rejection of almost every human feeling. When the stress from a frustrating endless divorce dragging on for months was added to my depression, the depression created physical symptoms.At first my nose twitched, then half my face, and finally painful neuralgia shot through the left side of my face. Fearful that I was suffering from post-polio syndrome from the illness I had had as a child, I went to see a neurologist. That doctor probed me physically and then psychologically. When I broke down in tears, to my horror and my surprise, he gave me the best advice I would receive during the recovery period, "Deal with your feelings or you will continue to feel this pain."

I began to talk about my feelings and the abuse. I began to see a family therapist who was more like a friend than my idea of what a therapist should be. Although I would like to be able to say that I immediately felt better, I didn't. The feelings I had denied started coming alive. The hurt, anger, sadness, fear, rejection, shame, blame, and hostility simmered up and flared. I seethed; I hurt; I cried. I was tossing on an angry sea of emotion. But eventually the waves subsided and the happy, joyous feelings started to emerge.

As painful as feeling and dealing with the feelings were, I felt alive. I was no longer depressed by what I couldn't feel. I was alive.

During this process the facial twitching and neuralgia subsided and eventually disappeared. Only occasionally now, during a tense moment, does my nose twitch and now I can read it as a physical symptom of some psychological tension, tension which when defined, can be addressed.

WHY TALKING ABOUT FEELINGS IS TRANSFORMATIVE

A woman recovering from an abusive relationship must feel her feelings and pay attention to them. A woman who has left an abusive relationship must talk about her experience of abuse. Telling others is transformative. Telling others about your experience and the feelings you had during the abuse and feel now is a way to move through the shame and secrecy that keep you isolated. Talking about the abuse also helps you work through denial of the truth of your experience and acknowledge the truth of your abuse. If you don't talk about it with others, you will not get understanding and help. You need that understanding and help to heal. You may not be able to heal totally on your own. You need others listening to you, responding to you, reaching out to you with love to heal.

By telling others about your abuse, you will get in touch with your feelings. You will get a chance to see your experience and yourself through the compassionate eyes of a supporter. You need not feel that you are all alone anymore. By sharing your experience openly with others, you will allow for the kind of intimacy that comes from honesty. This intimacy is the basis for friendship and for true growth on your part. By being able to discuss the abuse of your past, you are also establishing yourself as a person in the present who is dealing with something bad from the past. You are growing beyond the abuse, and eventually you will feel proud and strong that you were able to deal with it, grow, and become the person you always wanted to be. Finally, you will be a model for other women. Someone close to you may be experiencing abuse right now, and keeping it a secret from you. A woman is abused every 16 seconds in this country. You may become a model for someone else, and will join a courageous group of women who no longer feel they must suffer in silence.

You will not choose to act on all your feelings, but to deny them is to deny the living part of our spirits. To begin to heal, to get on to living again, to keep on living consciously and joyously, we must know what we are feeling. Feelings are the facts of our inner world. Nathaniel Branden in his book <u>The Psychology of Romantic Love</u>, writes, "We stay alive, psychologically, by staying in touch with our feelings, with our emotions, with our thoughts and longings and fantasies and judgments --with everything that pertains to the world of inner experience."

THE NEED FOR THERAPY

I have briefly described one of the ways we can deal with our feelings about the experience of abuse, through therapy. Therapy is essential in the early stages of recovery. I cannot emphasize enough the need to see a professional therapist. Abuse is heavy business and needs to be dealt with by a professional. Support groups for victims of abuse are good too, but need to be coupled with one-on-one therapy just for you.

A good therapist may take some searching out on your part. Referrals from friends or your doctor are a good place to start. Once you have a therapist in mind, make an appointment. Sometimes the first visit can be a consultation (no charge) and you can ask questions about the license or certification of the therapist, how long they have been practicing, and the approach to be used. Also find out about their cancellation policy, fees, and payment schedule, and availability to you in a crisis. You should check your health insurance. Many states have mandated that health insurance must provide a minimum amount for mental health benefits so some or all of the fees may be covered. Check with your insurance company to see if they will cover the particular therapist you have in mind. If they are not state certified, the insurance may not cover the visit. These steps will help you maintain a long-term relationship with the therapist that best suits you. Invest the time it takes to do these things to maximize the investment you are making in yourself. A good therapist will respect your efforts to make the most suitable arrangements to meet your needs and will help you if they are a professional.

A good therapist should feel like a friend, someone you trust who is helping you learn. My therapist did not show up for my first consultation but called immediately and apologized. She had gotten her schedule confused. She won me over to return by giving me two free visits and noting that I had learned that she too was human. She never pretended to be someone with all the answers. In fact, her approach was to ask questions and reflect back by answers to help me hear myself.

A survivor of domestic abuse should probably choose a female therapist. At this point in your recovery, you and another female will have an easier time establishing trust. Later on, it may be appropriate to try a male therapist to work through male-female issues, but right now you need to trust your therapist and feel safe.

WRITING AS A THERAPY TOOL

Over the longer term, we must learn how to deal with our feelings ourselves since feelings are generated every instant that we are alive. Our feelings are our alive part. They indicate how we are feeling and we can be motivated to change something in our outer world to feel better. They tell us about ourselves, our desires, needs, what we want to do, our dreams. Our feelings don't need to control us. We can choose how to react to them, observe them, and detach from them if appropriate. But if we ignore them, we won't be reacting consciously from our true center.

Being a writer by nature, I discovered that writing in my journal was a powerful tool to discover what my feelings were. I have always kept a journal, off and on. At some stages of my life, I have kept a diary, and written in it religiously everyday. When I started writing seriously in my journal after my separation, I was surprised that when I picked up the pen to write, the words literally flowed out. It was as if I was not really writing; the pen was guided by my spirit and my heart and not my hand. What was even more surprising was when I reread my entries, my feelings were very clearly revealed. I was amazed to read the entries and see how strong the feelings were: anger, shame, joy, pain, sorrow, pride, concern, love, hurt, guilt. The feelings rolled out of the words and lay exposed to me. I began to see that journal writing was a way of seeing inside myself and I used it deliberately.

When I discussed how effective writing was in understanding what I was feeling, my therapist suggested that I use the technique more deliberately, and combine it with an ability of mine to see images. She asked me to write my feelings by using images and see if I found that helpful. The entry at the beginning of this chapter was such an attempt on my part. I wrote about the way I isolated myself from my husband to protect myself from him. After I had written about the box image, I was able to begin to knock the box down slowly. I used the box image for months. One summer day as I changed my clothes in my bedroom after work, I remember looking out into my backyard to admire my flowers and seeing my neighbor's house. For the first time since I had moved in, I really saw my neighbor's house and I suddenly realized that the box had been not just an image but a reality. I had really built walls around myself as self-protection, and as I looked past my immediate neighbor's yard, into the next, I realized I was seeing the neighborhood for the first time.

That first glimpse of the neighborhood was the beginning of my journey back to the living world from my own self-built sanctuary. The irony of the sanctuary is though it protected me, the feelings I was trying not to feel kept me locked in a prison which was just as damaging as the abuse I was trying to shut out.

I think that dealing with my feelings has always been a somewhat tentative act on my part. I was never sure that my feelings were valid. I always thought they were the wrong things to feel, that I was defective in what I felt. Even as a young girl, when I wrote my feelings into my journal, I was secretive, hiding my journal in my desk under the bottom drawer. I was afraid that my mother and sisters would see them, and the shame of having my feelings read by someone else was overwhelming.

Now as an adult woman, the friendships I value the most are those with people who talk openly about their feelings, and who listen closely to me talk about mine. As a young girl, I yearned for reassurance that my feelings were okay, that I didn't have to keep them hidden, that I could talk about them openly. Now of course, I know that to get that reassurance you have to share your feelings first. I talk to friends, about what is going on with me emotionally. I try to talk about my feelings sooner than I used to, but I still find it hard to do that. Finally, after I have wrestled with a feeling as long as I can stand, and I have shared it, I am always surprised by the relief that I feel. Exposed to the light of day, they are normal human feelings. They are not monsters when they come out, only when they stay in.

Keeping a journal, a log of emotions, is healthy and will help you understand your emotional world. Converting that feeling into an image may be an even stronger tool for you if you like to write. If you don't like to write, then I suggest you verbalize that image to your friends when discussing your feelings.

NETWORK OF FRIENDS

It is vital that you nurture a network of supportive friends who are truly interested in you and what you think and feel. This network is what will give you the friendship you need not only to heal but to live joyously. You should tend your friendship network as seriously as you tend a garden, planting new friends, weeding out the old that aren't good for your garden, and keeping the old faithfuls watered and fertilized.

Some people are capable of sustaining a huge network of friends, but some people need only a select few. My friends go back to every period of my life; one from each location or stage of my life. I work hard to keep in contact with them. I write letters; every time I receive a letter back, I have a special wicker shelf to put it on, and when I feel like writing I pick out the letters, and write the ones I owe, rereading their letters so I can recall what they too are doing and feeling. I have a couple of friends that I call on the phone frequently. Even though it is long distance, I have always felt a good long heart to heart talk is cheap therapy and I don't mind paying the bill. If you are to get past opening pleasantries and if you are to maintain an intimate friendship, you need to share the details of your life.

I have a friend that I discovered accidentally that I use basically as a sounding board for my feelings. We have an occasional lunch, and the real point of our relationship is that I can share with her; she can share with me, and we affirm each other. Sometimes we may confront, gently and with love and compassion, but in an affirming friendship, even that is affirmation; it is affirmation that we are worth being honest with each other.

FEELINGS AS GUIDE POSTS

The value of dealing with and feeling your emotions goes beyond the feeling. It is what we do with this information. If we are to live consciously, and joyously, we must guide our lives. To know what makes up happy, we have to know how we feel when we are experiencing life. It all sounds so simple: feel your feelings and use them as a guide for how to live. But I never trusted my own internal information, and then for long periods, I shut down my internal information to survive. I was afraid of anger especially because I was angry that I was treated with such disregard by people who should have cared how I felt, and if I had dealt with the anger, I would have gotten out sooner.

For women who have been abused, the need to feel and deal with feelings is essential. For someone who has not been in a dysfunctional system, the advice may seem self-serving and selfish. I don't think someone from a shame-based family system is ever selfish. They are on the opposite ends of the continuum. They have given up all their basic human rights to make the relationship better.

Knowing what they feel and acting on feelings put them in the middle of the continuum, which would look something like this.

> **Dysfunctional:** Give it all up to keep the other person happy; react; deny; doing these things will keep the relationship going; ignore your needs so that the other person will be happy.

> **Normal:** Trust your feelings. If you feel something isn't healthy, it probably isn't. Give the relationship time to develop so you can lower your boundaries gradually as trust is earned. If the other person is healthy, you will be able to negotiate to get your and their needs met in a mutually satisfactory way.

An abuser is not normal, rather dysfunctional, in his demands on you. The abuser wants you to give up everything for him. What they want is paramount. They will do whatever they have to do to get their needs met without regard for the mutuality of the relationship. They will manipulate you and situations to achieve fulfillment.

It is not selfish to feel an emotion and expect it to be validated by someone close to you. If you are wild with joy over some happy event, you should be able to emote about it, be proud about it, and the close person should too. If you are grief-stricken over something, you should have that close person be sympathetic and nurturing while you come to terms with your loss or setback. Only dysfunctional people expect you to be circumspect about your joy and neutral about your pain. We are human! God gave us feelings as guide posts. Read them and negotiate through the course of life based on that information. Until you do, you will not be living consciously and completely.

RECOMMENDATIONS FOR FURTHER WORK

1. Locate a therapist. Make an appointment and get into counselling as soon as possible.

2. Develop a network of supportive friends. Make a list of all the people you feel are nurturing. Cultivate friendships consciously.

3. Start a journal and write in it daily, focusing on how you feel.

CHAPTER FIVE

AFFIRM YOURSELF

It is not easy to treat yourself as something valuable when you really don't feel that way about yourself. I certainly did not feel that way for many years. When I was finally free of abuse, I didn't start treating myself with respect right away. I worked myself past exhaustion; I put off eating if I was busy even though I was hungry. I stayed up late finishing chores or studying or paying bills even though I was tired. I felt guilty when I bought myself anything; it didn't even have to be pretty clothes or nice things. I didn't expect anything of other people. I didn't ask other people to treat me with respect, and I rarely voiced a preference.

I did not see myself for what I really was. My talents, my personality, my thoughts, my feelings and dreams were all discounted. I discounted them because I had been told verbally, physically, and emotionally that I was nothing. After hundreds of shaming interactions, I had internalized those beliefs about myself. So, although I certainly had much to offer the world and others, I didn't feel that way about myself. To compensate for those negative feelings, I pushed myself past my physical limits to achieve. I was always achieving because it made me feel good about myself. The problem was that I had to keep on achieving, always, all the time, to maintain those good feelings. It was impossible to just be myself and relax.

Even the way I viewed my body was distorted. I had a problems buying clothes in the right size because when I looked in the mirror, I saw someone much heavier. I would try on an outfit, think it fit, and when I got home discover that it was too big. I had shrunk on my way home from the store! A good friend said to me once, "You don't get it, do you?" I said, "Get what?" She said, "That you're so very pretty, so vivacious and attractive." I didn't get it.

When I decided to go for life rather than bitterness, I decided to affirm myself, to affirm my life. I couldn't change the past but I could change the future. I decided I wanted to go for living life with joy, with caring for myself, with enthusiasm for my hopes and dreams or the damage I had experienced would continue to happen. Even if I wasn't married to an abusive husband, I was still married to disrespect and to shame. I had internalized those beliefs to such an extent that I was now doing it to myself.

I did overcome those shaming interactions. I take care of myself now, mentally, physically, spiritually, emotionally. I see my physical self accurately. I still work hard, but I play a lot more, and can actually do nothing if that's what I want to do. The ability to relax, to feel that I don't have to be all things to all people, to just be me has been the most precious gift to myself that I could have given myself. Life is so much more enjoyable when you believe these things.

AFFIRMING YOURSELF IS SELF-LOVE

Affirming yourself is an attitude about yourself that is based on self-love. You have to believe that you, like every human being, are different, unique and special. You don't have to be rich or famous to be special. We are all special. Each person has a personality like no one else's. Each of us thinks differently and acts differently.

Think about this concept by thinking of people you have loved who have died. What do you remember about them? The way their eyes twinkled just before they told a joke. That they loved gaudy pins and wore them with flair. That they loved to belong to organizations and be part of the group in some capacity such as secretary or president. That their hair was a distinctive shade of red and curled in a special way around their ears. As I write these words, I am thinking of my eighth grade English teacher, Mrs. Lillian Zahn. I loved her because she was herself. She believed in me and told me many times that I was special. She encouraged me "to just be myself." Did I love her because she was rich, famous, and beautiful. No way! She wasn't any of those things. I loved her because she was Lillian Zahn, unique in this world. I didn't see her after eighth grade, and she died a few years later, but I could recreate her for you by writing several thousand words about her. I've never met anyone like her since.

Your friends, if they have the talent of writing, could do the same about you. And in doing so, they would touch on what you say, what makes you laugh or cry, what you love or hate, how you look, walk and sound. But they might never mention your accomplishments or lack of accomplishments. Their portrait would be the essence of you, that unknowable spirit that is born into the human body and passes out of the body when we die.

To heal from abuse, you absolutely must believe this concept--that you just as you are--are valuable.

MESSAGES TO SELF

Interrupt your stream of consciousness for a moment and listen to what you are right now saying about yourself. Are you shocked and dismayed about what you believe about yourself? Some of these messages might sound like this:

--Really, I am no good.
--I don't deserve to be happy.
--I am unlovable.
--I always make mistakes. I can't do anything right.
--You wouldn't say that if you really knew me
--I shouldn't have said that. It was a dumb remark.
--No one likes me.
--No one loves me.

Do these sound familiar? By saying these negative statements to yourself, you're reinforcing the negative messages you've learned from others in dysfunctional relationships. You have to reprogram your mind to replace negative messages with positive self-affirmations. Your unconscious says yes to everything you tell it. Tell yourself good things about yourself in a positive way and your subconscious will accept the statement.

Start with these positive self-affirmations:

--I am good enough.
--I am special.
--I deserve to be happy.
--I am lovable just as I am.
--I am an attractive human being.

--It's okay to make mistakes. I don't have to be perfect.
--People like me the way I am. Be myself and I'll be fine.
--I have many friends.
--I am loved my others.
--The world is a safe and nurturing place.
--I can trust myself and what I feel.
--I can choose to see the best in this situation.
--Everything will be okay. I have everything I need to get through this.
--I am valuable just as I am.

Every time you hear yourself tear yourself down, call out your coach, the self-affirmation cheerleader, and shout back a self-affirmation. Select one or two and write them down and paste them on your mirror, put them in your desk drawer at work, and on the back side of your kitchen cupboard. Say them over and over to yourself.

Believe the messages. Start with moments, turn them into minutes, then hours. Their power will amaze you. By consciously tuning into our inner voice, we can change the anger, blame, contempt, and criticism to respect, tenderness, valuing of self and forgiveness of our mistakes and failings.

READ MATERIALS THAT EMPHASIZE SELF-ESTEEM

In addition to saying self-affirmations whenever we hear our inner voice disparaging our self, we can supplement our reading material with reading materials that emphasize this tender, valuing approach to ourselves. The Hazelden Foundation in conjunction with Harper & Row Publishers publishes many meditation books to assist codependents in their recovery. Originally developed for people recovering from drug and alcohol addictions, these books can help anyone interested in growing. Some of the titles include:

<u>The Promise of a New Day</u>, <u>Each Day a New Beginning:
Daily Meditations for Women</u> and more. These books belong on your reading table, in your purse, in your desk. During a triggering incident, when the inner voice is shouting negative messages louder than you can whisper back, reading some of these passages will get you back on a smoother keel so that you can again hear yourself whisper good things, and believe them.

TAKE CARE OF YOUR BODY

There are many other aspects of affirming our self. We can start with another basic home plate, our bodies. If you are eating well, exercising regularly, and getting enough sleep, you are bound to feel better about yourself because you are allowing yourself to make and store the energy and stamina a person needs to live happily. If you are filling your body with junk foods and not allowing your body to cleanse the chemicals it makes when stressed, you are going to feel lousy. It is almost impossible to feel depressed if you have done something that allows your heart to pump your blood through your body vigorously. The blood is going to go through your internal organs and be cleansed of all the chemicals that have been released by stress and tension.

The physical activity doesn't have to kill you with the exertion. A brisk walk around the neighborhood or through a park three times a week for twenty minutes will make you feel better. You could bicycle, swim, dance, ride an exercise bicycle, whatever suits your lifestyle and interests. You can vary the exercise. But you must do it. If you're not an early bird, do it after supper, or during your lunch hour. Make yourself be physical for a month. Say to yourself that you'll try it for that long, and if you don't feel better, you won't continue. I guarantee that you will start to feel better. You won't feel as depressed; you will feel more relaxed. You may even find there's a spring in your step and a bloom in your cheek from the exercise. The benefits to your

Affirm Yourself 51

mental health will be matched by the benefits to your physical health. But you must do it to experience them.

Read some of the many magazine and newspaper articles on exercise to better educate yourself on the benefits. Look for ideas that will work for you. Maybe a competitive activity is appealing. Maybe something you can do anytime by yourself is attractive. Maybe you need a friend exercising with you. Maybe you need to exercise alone.

Keep looking and you'll find something you like enough to stick with it over a long period of time.

Along with exercise, examine your diet. Are you making enough time for good eating in your life. Eating lots of fruits, vegetables, and grains doesn't really take more time but it does take planning. Figure out some simple dishes that are made from wholesome ingredients that appeal to your palate and that you enjoy. Treat yourself well in the food area and you will feel better in the mind as well. A body is like a furnace. It needs fuel to run efficiently. Don't expect yourself to run all day on coffee and cigarettes. Plan for your calories to be as enjoyable as any other activity. Chances are you'll find that when you pay closer attention to your diet, you feel better, maybe lose a few extra pounds, and more importantly, have the energy to do all the things you want to do.

Even in those areas of exercise and diet, the better you treat yourself, the better others treat you. If you think you're special enough to fuss over and give yourself nutritious meals and planned exercise activity, you're well on the way to recovery.

OTHER WAYS TO AFFIRM SELF

There are literally dozens of other ways to affirm yourself. For instance, how you dress can have an impact on how you feel about yourself. Look your best. If you feel beautiful, you are beautiful. One of the small ways I started affirming myself was by buying myself new clothes. At first, it was just one thing at a time, and not necessarily expensive things, but these were clothes that I truly wanted, and which made me look special too. Several years into my recovery, I went for a weekend with two bosom buddies. We went to a fancy hotel in Chicago, attended the opera, and we shopped, and shopped, and shopped. With their encouragement, I spent a lot of money on new additions to my wardrobe. I even spent a small fortune on a silk scarf to match my new clothes, and then of course I needed a pin, a purse, and earrings to go along with the scarf.

Rationally, I know it was extravagant for me, but not out of line with my pocketbook. The important thing was that I had never, ever bought as many beautiful and expensive things for myself at the same time. Did I feel guilty? Yes, a little bit, but I discovered that every time I wore those clothes, I felt good. I felt beautiful and I felt pampered.

Affirming yourself is an attitude. It is asking yourself, "What do I need right now?" when you feel sad, depressed, or forlorn. And then trying to give it to yourself. Affirming yourself is making every activity a pleasant one. Buying scented soaps and using them for bathing and washing your hands sends the delicate fragrance to your nose and you feel nurtured. Cutting a flower from your garden or buying even one flower and putting it in your home delights your visual sense and tells you that you are special. Having a special chair to read in gives you a place to relax and unwind. Arranging your drawers and cupboards and closets so that they are orderly and you can work efficiently and find things without being constantly frustrated is nurturing. Having special music you like playing while you iron or scrub a floor is taking care of yourself. We owe it to ourselves to make every minute of our lives the best they can be. Even in these small ways we affirm ourselves.

There is nothing wrong with doing pampering activities for yourself. These are affirming your self-

Affirm Yourself

worth by making yourself feel good. Some of the ways I pamper myself are to give myself a manicure at least once a week, have my hair done as often as possible, go to the kind of movies that make me laugh, and spend weekends at my cabin in the country. Or I call up my best friend in Seattle and talk to her when I miss her or go out to lunch with someone special.

Once I started being good to myself, I found it a lot harder to feel sorry for myself. I could take a nice hot bath or snuggle down with a good book or go for a spontaneous bicycle ride with my kids and thoughts of how hard I had it were chased out of my mind.

When I started counselling, my therapist would ask me what I wanted. I honestly couldn't answer her. It had been so long since I'd asked myself what I wanted that I didn't know. It had been so long since someone asked me what I wanted, that I didn't know. Today, if you asked me what I wanted, I could tell you 230 things at least, and probably go on from there.

I recently went to an outdoor crafts fair. One booth specializing in wood carvings offered a pair of whittled sunfish for $13.00. I really wanted to buy those sunfish. I could see them hanging on the porch of my lake cabin. But the price seemed high and when I bargained, the seller wouldn't reduce the price. I walked away. Then I decided that paying a few more dollars for those sunfish wouldn't break the bank, so I went back and bought them. I like those sunfish. They remind me of fishing for sunfish as a child, and they were worth the price. But in another time, I would have foregone them --nobly out of a sense of prudence and deeper out of a sense that I wasn't worth the money. Self-esteem, a belief that you are worthy, of value just as you are, is a fundamental building block to happiness. It is not selfishness, not vanity to believe you are unique, valuable, and lovable. It is vital that you believe that. Believing you are worthy does not mean you don't try to improve. In fact, if you don't believe that you won't be motivated to improve.

FAKE IT IF YOU HAVE TO

If after reading this chapter on affirming yourself, and you'd like to believe it but can't, I urge you to fake it. Fake it that you like yourself; go ahead and act that way even if you have your doubts. I firmly believe that if you fake it long enough and hard enough, you will begin to feel the difference between valuing and caring for yourself and disparaging and criticizing yourself. The difference will feel kind of nice, and you may see a glimmer now and then of what it's like to expect others to treat you well, and how they respond to that attitude. You'll probably find that you're having a lot more fun, and laughing more than you used to. You may even find that you enjoy being alive, and that getting up and facing each day's problems and responsibilities isn't as hard.

Turning around an attitude about yourself that you've had drummed in you by your former spouse or significant other is hard to do, but it is worth it and it can be done.

Keep on trying; you're worth the effort!

RECOMMENDATIONS FOR FURTHER WORK

1. Make a list of affirming activities. Everyday do one of those activities at a minimum. Make yourself a daily chart and track yourself. Then affirm yourself at the end of the month in a big way for affirming yourself.

2. Everyday read an affirmation and say it over and over. Establish a discipline to verbal affirmations. For instance, always say them when you brush your teeth, do dishes, or say your prayers.

3. Keep in mind that looking good makes you feel good about yourself. Spend time on your appearance. Treat yourself to new clothes, accessories or jewelry. Take time to dress. When you look in the mirror, give yourself a compliment.

CHAPTER SIX

CAREER PLANNING GIVES YOU CONTROL

You need to take charge of your life to be in control of your present and future. Establishing economic independence is one of the steps you can take. It's insurance that you will not end up dependent on someone who is not good to you or good for you. If you do not want history to repeat itself, the ability to provide a decent standard of living for yourself and children can go a long way towards creating a happy life.

Having choices is freedom. Economic independence gives you choices. That is not to say that powerful and financially independent women aren't ever abused. Statistics show it crosses all economic classes. However, economic independence will prevent a woman who has healthy self-esteem from being locked into a miserable life.

Economic independence also helps raise self-esteem. Providing for yourself and family is something to take pride in, and adds to your feelings of self-worth. As the saying goes, nothing succeeds like success. Nothing feels as good as providing a good life for yourself.

As long as you must work, expand your thinking beyond having a job into having a job that is a career. A career is the high road to independence and control. It gives you choices as well as opportunities to develop your talents and abilities to make an exciting, satisfying life rather than being a prisoner in what appears to be the only way to live.

When I was in my abusive marriage, my husband was opposed to my working outside the home. When I did earn my real estate license, he went out of his way to prevent me from continuing in the field. He would not allow me to buy a second car which I could use; lucky for me, I was fortunate enough to inherit an automobile, old but in good running order. It allowed me access to the world outside my home. He would not help with running the household in any way. He threw a fit when I had to work floor time on weekends. When I became pregnant, he breathed a visible sigh of relief because of his expectation that I would now stay home. I did, and I felt trapped, that there was no way out. No money to escape on, no close family to run to, no refuge house to go to for safety, I had to stay until I was able to get up the courage to leave no matter what the obstacles were.

It was a lot easier to walk out the second time, knowing I had a way to provide for myself and children. I didn't walk out because I was economically independent. I walked out because I had choices about how I was choosing to live my life. One of the reasons men are threatened by women who are successful and thriving on their own resources is that these women do have choices and no longer have to be dependent. Of course, a man with healthy self-esteem wants a woman who is thriving and developing and producing and contributing in whatever way her talents lead her, but that is another story.

JOB AND CAREER DEFINED

If you look up the word job in the dictionary, you'll see it comes from Middle English, originally meaning mouthful. The dictionary defines job as a piece of work, anything one has to do, or a position of employment. A job supports you, pays the bills, puts food on the table, but is something you're eager to leave at the end of the working day. On the other hand, the word career derives from the Latin word meaning wagon road or path. The dictionary gives several definitions, including one's progress through life; one's advancement or achievement in a particular vocation; a lifework; profession; occupation. People such as doctors, lawyers, writers, teachers, and news broadcasters are described as having careers.

There is a difference between career and job. Individual jobs over a period of time can add up to a career if there is linkage between skills and knowledge used. But often jobs are just positions of employment. You could waitress at an endless number of restaurants and still be a waitress. You could type an endless number of letters and still be a clerk/typist. The difference between career and a job is also accentuated by the feeling of satisfaction you derive from the work. In addition, there are usually differences in pay because jobs are at the low end of the totem pole. There is also a difference in stature and status. A career gives you pride, reflecting your progress in life.

The number of careers are endless. One can have a career in law enforcement, in office administration, as an accountant, in the food services business, or in engineering to name a few.

Some careers are based on distinct bodies of knowledge that must be acquired in order to practice: such as medicine, law, real estate. Those careers are more accurately called professions and often require passing examinations that measure whether you have the required knowledge and/or adherence to a code of ethics.

A career is the building up of skills and knowledge from position to position, overlapping to create expertise and broad and specific knowledge in a paid position. For example, a job as a typist leading to a position as an administrative secretary leading to a position as an office administrator is a career.

ELEMENTS IN A CAREER

Several elements must be present to have a career. The first element is a steady progression from one position to another which builds on the knowledge and skills used in that position for knowledge and skills needed in the next. There is a pattern to the positions and they complete a person's understanding of a particular area so that they have a broad understanding of a certain field. The symbol of an upside down pyramid conceptualizes this concept. Each step up builds on previous layers so that at the top you understand most aspects of a selected field. If you, when you graduated from college, took a job as a public relations assistant, you would have mastered the techniques of writing press releases and developing mailing lists. When you got promoted to media representative, you learned how to communicate with the media and answer their questions. You may have then advanced to working on annual and quarterly financial reports for the company. By the time you became a manager, you had done most of the discrete tasks in the work unit so you had an indepth as well as broad understanding of the work of the department.

A commonly made mistake is to jump from one job to another without looking for linkages of skills and knowledge between positions of employment. Employers look for linkages between job requirements and candidate skills and knowledge when they hire. They are more willing to hire a candidate for a fulltime secretarial position in the benefits department who had a previous position doing correspondence and routine typing as well as benefits work. That new secretarial position specializing in benefits might then lead to an entry level benefits administration position, which could lead up a career path.

Some skills are universal and apply to most jobs. These include planning and organizing skills, communicating, both oral and written, working with others, and the ability to assert your opinions without alienating others. Other important skills are the ability to learn and solve problems. Your ability to innovate and be creative will also serve you well. Almost everyone today has to use a computer to do some part of their job. Word processing skills are used by everyone as personal computers become an office fixture. They are used in manufacturing production to control equipment, by accountants, secretaries, engineers to design, and writers to do desktop publishing.

Those universal skills and the specific technical and job knowledge you have in a field will help you build a career when you look for the linkages between the skills you have and the job requirements.

The second element for a career is a natural interest and talent and desire to do the work required of the position. When you want to do something rather than have to do something, you are able to take the bad with the good. You bring an energy to the work that drives you to do your best, to keep going when you feel discouraged or overwhelmed by the challenge. You work for the challenge and excitement that the position can give. While no position is always exciting, and rewarding, and work is called work because it takes our energy, the general feeling of a careerist is satisfaction and interest in the work. You feel like you are contributing and you enjoy doing it. If you do not feel this way, something about the work goes against your natural tendencies and interests and creates tension for you.

You will never be as successful doing something you don't enjoy as you will doing something you enjoy. You must have your heart in it to do your best.

When I was in college, I got a part-time job as a clerical helper for a catering firm. To say that I hated it is an understatement. The pay was okay and the employers were friendly, but the office was tiny, dimly lit, and cramped. I worked two feet away from the owners. My duties included answering the phone and answering questions on their catering services, which I had not been trained to do, and did not understand. I despised that. I added up their bills and prepared invoices. I'm not very good at that sort of detail work and I disliked it for that reason. Finally I had to type letters and I found that boring and monotonous. I quit because I couldn't stand the work. It was obviously not my line of work. I then went out and got a job as a student helper in a department at the university doing xeroxing, mimeographing, and dittoing. I worked independently, providing services to the faculty and students, and enjoyed the tasks and atmosphere. I was able to go to various rooms where the equipment was located and worked with very little supervision. I stayed there until I graduated.

CAREER PLANNING ISSUES FOR WOMEN

Career planning is difficult for both men and women. But for women, career planning is more complicated because of the particular issues women face. Men don't have babies and therefore don't need to deal with the questions those children introduce into women's lives. Women must plan for and manage the interruptions those children bring. Women have only recently viewed career planning as a key question in their lives. Men have always identified very closely with their work. For women, the question of what to do with their lives has often been answered by the people in their lives rather than themselves. Husbands and children place demands. Many women never question that they should be asking "what is it I want?" when making decisions based on the events of their lives.

The truth of the matter is that you probably plan better menus and social activities than you plan your career. This reactionary stance on career planning prevents you from finding out what you really want to do with your life, and robs you of fulfillment, achieving your potential, satisfaction, and higher levels of income.

IDEAL CAREER PLANNING

Ideally career planning does not look at work as a separate activity into which all the energy and drive is poured and personal and family aspects of life are sacrificed. Career planning can accommodate other needs and strives for balance in all the areas that make life fulfilling: home, community, religious activity, personal interests as well as work. You can have it all, just not all at the same time.

Career planning takes a long term view of life and recognizes that there are life stages. Each stage may meet one need but not another. However, over the long run, you as a whole have achieved your goals. Career planning helps interruptions become pauses along the path. Remember there is no one right path except the path we create and choose for ourselves.

Career planning presupposes that the purpose of career planning is not to reach high, but also to broaden and deepen knowledge and skills and personal contributions to achieve life satisfaction. With the baby boom generation all competing for the same positions, with companies shrinking their workforces, opportunities to move up in the organization are decreasing. Therefore taking a broader view insures your satisfaction, the true measure of success, when the external measures of success may be limited.

HOW TO DETERMINE CAREER DIRECTION

Interests and values are a good guide for direction setting in career choices. By tapping into your natural talents which are generally displayed in your interests, you can find career choices that tap into the things you want to succeed at. Because it is a natural match, you will be motivated to achieve because it is satisfying. Think back to the things you have done that have been so absorbing and rewarding that you worked on the tasks for hours without being aware of the passage of time or your body's needs. Those are the activities that will truly engage you and keep you motivated.

Do you like working with things? Working with people? Or working with data? No job is all one or the other, but jobs can be categorized generally into one of these three categories.

Verbs that describe working with things include: precision work, setting up, manipulating, controlling, operating, handling, tending, building. Jobs that deal primarily with things are, for example, auto mechanic, farmer, truck driver, painter, and seamstress. Working with things can be working with big things or little things, each different. Mechanics work with big things; a jeweler works with tiny parts and small tools. Look to your hobbies to see if this applies.

Do people give you energy? Do you like helping them or would your prefer to work alone? Working with people could be further broken down into working with large groups of people at a time, or working individually with people. A classroom teacher would be an example of someone working with groups of people whereas a medical doctor, though he/she sees hundreds of people a day, works with each of them individually, one at a time. Verbs that describe working with people include mentoring, negotiating, supervising, consulting, instructing, treating, coaching, persuading, helping, serving, exchanging information. Some job examples are teacher, counsellor, minister, receptionist, salesperson, union organizer, supervisor, to name a few.

Do you like working with data, information, facts and figures. If you like data, working with people can be an annoyance, but if you like people, working with data can be frustrating. Verbs that describe data jobs are analyzing, computing, compiling, counting, copying, and comparing. Jobs that deal primarily with data include software analyst, file clerk, bookkeeper, typist, proofreader, accountant, cashier, as examples.

There are other definite personality orientations which can also guide you in your career choices. Patterns for personalities are based on how we prefer to perceive information and how we prefer to make decisions based on that information.

You can perceive information about the world from the information from your senses. A sensory orientation is based on awareness of experience, good powers of observation and a memory for facts and details. Or you can get your information from the insight of intuition. Intuition is a sixth sense, a hunch, a feeling of relearning something you already know. Intuition provides the ability to see abstract, symbolic and theoretical relationships and deal with complexity. Our information-gathering orientation combined with how we make decisions creates a personality orientation.

If when you make a decision, you are analytical, and logical, sticking to the facts, you will come to a different conclusion than if you interact with the information personally, considering how you would feel, or how it impacts the individual. If you are a logical thinker combined with liking the facts based on the world around you, you would find your talents well used in the technical field with facts and objects as your goal.

If you prefer the facts from the world around you, but tend to be sympathetic and friendly about those facts, your talents might lie in health care, community service, sales, and teaching, where you could work with people.

If, on the other hand, you are intuitive and focus on possibilities and the overall picture, rather than details, combined with being logical and analytical in your approach to decisions, then going into theoretical and technical fields would draw upon your talents. Fields such as physical science, research, and management would be attractive to you. If on the other hand, the possibilities and overall view were handled with the personal touch, you would probably find that you understand and communicate well with people. Therefore the fields of behavioral science, literature and the arts would be attractive to you and use your talents well.

Both your values and orientation should also guide you in making some selections within your choice categories. You should give some thought to what kind of work characteristics would suit you best. Do you like a small company which gives closer working relationships, and less defined duties? Or would you prefer a larger, more impersonal organization with clearly defined rules and procedures? Do you like to get up in the morning knowing what you'll do that day? Or is having the unexpected happen exciting? Do you like to travel? Do you like to take risks or would you prefer to avoid them? Does working at a fast pace with deadlines and pressure for results excite you and make you thrive, or do you want to go at a steady and sure pace? Do you like to work independently or have others dependent on your work? Do financial rewards tied to your work results motivate you or would you prefer to get a regular paycheck without the highs and lows of variable income? Do you like to work on short projects and then go on to something new or do you want to work at something that continues indefinitely? These work characteristics play a role in determining how satisfied you'll be with your job in addition to the work content. You might like the basic work content, but find that you're in the situation of how you perform the job that affects your satisfaction.

I counselled a young man at work who did repair of equipment. The department he worked in processed computer chips and involved many different types of equipment. The department was critical to the rest of the manufacturing process flowing forward so whenever equipment broke down, it was a crisis. He also worked second shift, so when he came in there was usually a crisis occurring. He liked repairing equipment, but not with that kind of pressure on him. He had become so stressed by the work characteristics that he was becoming ill. His problem was alleviated when he transferred to a department where crisis was not an everyday occurrence and he worked as part of a team so that the total responsibility for repairing the equipment did not rest on his shoulders.

Even when you have made choices about what kind of work you like and how you like to do it, there is uncertainty. There are so many ways to fulfill some of your needs. Even when you know what those needs are, you might be able to do them in many different ways. It's similar to being in the middle of a maze and looking at dozens of possible ways to the end. A person who likes people could teach, work in a service industry or be a counsellor.

RESOURCES FOR CAREER PLANNING

Resources exist all around you to give you lots of data. Your personnel department at work should be able to provide you with some career counselling. Vocational schools and colleges usually offer free or minimally priced career counselling. There are private career counsellors you can pay to find out what you want to do.

A career counsellor can administer different types of instruments that can guide you on career choice. One of these instruments is the Myers-Briggs Type Inventory which tells your personality orientation based on perception and judgment processes. Your responses indicate your preferences, strengths and weaknesses. Another instrument is the Strong Interest Inventory. Based on your answers to many questions about your preferences, a computer printout suggests the kinds of occupations you are likely to prefer, the fields you should avoid, and the degree of similarity between your interest and those of employed people in many occupations. There are many other types of instruments that I have not discussed.

While these instruments are useful, any good career counsellor, test or instrument can only guide you. Ultimately only you can answer the question of what you want to do, like to do, and find satisfying.

Career planning involves looking at all areas of life to achieve balance and yet move forward on multiple fronts. By planning for yourself, you actively look out for your happiness. This proactive process requires knowing your talents, interests and personality orientation and requires work and time. The results however are the satisfaction from knowing yourself and using that knowledge to contribute to your own happiness and satisfaction as well as the community around you while getting paid for doing something you enjoy. This enhances your life and the lives of those in your life. This gives you choices so that you are free to choose how you want to live your whole life. This gives you control and puts the balance of power between a man and a woman in balance so that both are freely entering and staying in a relationship from mutual respect and love and not fear and intimidation.

BEHAVIORS THAT WILL MAKE YOU SUCCESSFUL

Careful thought and planning can go a long way to making you successful. In addition, there are some behaviors on the job that will guarantee your success on the job too. First of all, have a strong work ethic. All bosses like the employees who put in a full day's work for a day's pay. These employees are punctual, respect breaks and meal time starts and stops, and work, work, work. Plan your use of time so that is wisely spent. If you work hard, you'll be productive and all bosses know who their most productive employees are.

If you remember, too, that by making your boss look good, you'll look good, you'll also succeed. Make your boss's job as easy as you can. If you don't understand what you are supposed to do, ask questions. If you have a suggestion, make it. Then let your boss decide if it should be implemented. Express yourself clearly and courteously, and you'll find that you will get approached by your boss for your opinions and suggestions. Strive to take a problem-solving approach to problems. The employee who tries to help solve problems rather than suffer frustration and fail to find solutions will demonstrate a winning attitude.

Be flexible about change. This decade will be no different from the last. Changes will need to be made. Someone who is willing to try something and give it a fair trial, or come up with a better way of working will be a better partner than someone who is always ready to fight every change and put up roadblocks. Being adaptable will help you progress. The adaptable employees will be offered new opportunities. If you take them even in the face of risk, you will profit.

Think for yourself. Don't listen to the factory or office scuttlebutt or disgruntlement. In the long run, you will come out ahead by forming your own opinions and will receive recognition for your leadership abilities.

At the same time, make friends and network. Talk to the people you find always know what is really going on. They can provide you with helpful insights and information. Observe how other employees handle problems and situations and learn from those who are most successful at their jobs. You will learn how to solve problems in your company's environment.

Always keep learning. Learn formally through classes, either credit or non-credit. Take time to read in your field and keep up with current events as well. Be curious and feed your curiosity. Lifelong learning is necessary to advance in today's world with so much knowledge being added daily. If you keep learning, you'll never get outdated or rusty. You'll find you're more creative, better at problem-solving, and advancing on the job.

Finally, do the best job you can. The best way to get a promotion is to do the best job you can with the job you have now. The saying that you have to know the right people simply isn't true. Good workers get promoted. If you think you know what will happen next, think again. Employees quit, get fired, get promoted, and that creates a ripple effect. If you truly are good at your work, you'll get noticed.

By having a plan and being flexible about your career when change occurs, you will find that you are finding satisfaction and fulfillment in your work. You'll bring home a bigger paycheck, feel pride in your accomplishments, and you will be able to live independently on your own resources if you have to or want to. This gives you freedom through choices. This makes you feel good about yourself. Never again will you have to feel that you have to stay in an abusive relationship because you think you cannot make it on your own.

RECOMMENDATIONS FOR FURTHER WORK

1. Spend time thinking about your current job. Do you like it? What parts don't you like? Ask yourself all the questions from the chapter with the end goal of describing for yourself what your perfect job would be.

2. If you think you need some help getting the answers, make an appointment with some type of career counsellor to begin the process. You can find counsellors listed in the Yellow Pages under "Career and Vocational Counselling."

3. Visit your public library and read magazine articles and books on the subject.

4. Keep your resume updated. Even if you're not now looking for a new job, type up a new resume so that you'll be ready if something should come up. In the process of reviewing your past job history, education, and other accomplishments, you may learn something about your career direction.

5. Maintain a personal accomplishments file. Put in the clippings from your community and religious involvement. Save letters from your boss and others complimenting you on a job well done. If you take a class, put the grade report in your file so that you will remember to put it on your resume. Have a special place to save all the reminders of your past accomplishments.

CHAPTER SEVEN

GOALS: A POWERFUL TOOL

Goals are a powerful tool for taking charge of your life. The dreams you dream, the wishes you wish can become your reality through goals. Goals are powerful because goals channel your energy into the direction you have set. If you do not set direction, your energy will be dispersed in many different ways. By channeling your energy, you will get what you want.

I have always been a person who plans and I had achieved many things in my life. But it wasn't until I set goals that tapped into the things I really believed in that I became successful.

CORE VALUES

To truly achieve your dreams, wishes, and desires, you need to go through the process of figuring out your core values. Core values are the most important beliefs you hold. You may not be recovered enough to be easily in touch with your inner world. You may have to work to draw out your dreams and what truly matters to you. I am asking you to make conscious decisions about how you want to live the rest of your life rather than react to the circumstances of your life and be passive about choices. You may have deferred to others on choices for so long that this may not be easy. You may have let your husband or man in your life decide many of these important issues. You may feel so weighted down by your obligations and responsibilities that you think there is no room in your life for what you truly dream about and desire. "How can I?", you ask yourself, as you tend to your children, cook and clean, and go to work everyday to pay a steady stream of bills, "Pursue my dreams?"

Not to pursue your dreams and desires is the greatest disservice you can do yourself. You are denying the creative, human part of yourself. You will not feel good about yourself if you are not directing your life towards your creative impulses which flow from your dreams and desires. To pursue your dreams and desires feels good. It makes life tolerable where it might be intolerable when you feel your life is leading to the goals you desire. That is why men and women have been able to push their bodies and minds to new limits; they felt what they were doing was worthwhile.

Live with your heart, and you'll have the energy to do everything you want to do.

In the process of sifting through the messages inside, you want to focus on a half-dozen or less. I am talking about core values such as truth, justice, compassion, kindness, health, honesty, integrity and creativity, to name some that are important to me. As Robert Fritz says in his book, <u>The Path of Least Resistance</u>, this process changes you profoundly. "The standard of measurement in life shifts from emotional states to what is truly important and most worthy of you as a human being on this planet in this historic period. Your true satisfaction and fulfillment come from nothing short of this."

I can speak enthusiastically of this goal-setting process because I have been doing it and seeing unbelievable results, reaching 95% of my goals and pursuing my dreams. The first time I went through a thorough goal-setting process, I did not believe completely in the process. Two years later when I went back to check my progress, I was stunned to see that even the goals that I had considered wishful thinking had been achieved. I had written down as one of my goals that I wanted a cabin in the woods to retreat to for peace, recreation, and a place to write. Now I have one, and it was achieved without undue work and some luck because when I happened upon the cabin, I recognized it as something I truly wanted, and as an unexpected opportunity to fulfill that dream. I was able to act quickly on the sale to take advantage of a good buy.

I had also written down that I wanted each of my daughters to go to college to be prepared for meaningful careers. The financial part of that goal has been achieved. I have set aside a significant chunk of money for each of them to achieve that goal. There were other goals, sixteen in all. Only one has not been achieved: to relearn to play the piano. I don't think it taps into my dreams. When I went through the exercise again, I did not put it on my list.

I have learned that you do not have to be cautious and say to yourself that you will never achieve your dreams. Perhaps right now it is not clear to you how achieving your dream will look, but it if is based on a core value, something you believe in completely, you will

Goals 73

achieve that dream if you set a goal to do so. Be careful! You will!

The simple truth for me is that we as human beings derive our greatest sense of satisfaction from our accomplishments. We can all accomplish what we want to accomplish in life. The hard part is figuring out what that is and then the rest is easy. This formula for achieving satisfaction is simple: it's as simple as counting one, two, three. Don't be fooled by its simplicity. It is as powerful as a bomb exploding. This is how you do it.

STEP ONE OF THE FORMULA FOR ACHIEVING

You decide what you want in life. Sift through all the garbage messages you've received about what you should want, what society says you should want, what you tell yourself you want. Do you want to help other people? Do you want to be in tune with nature? Do you want to realize your intellectual potential? These are the elementary choices you need to make upon which to build your life, the core values that truly matter to you.

Here are some values you will want to consider in the process of deciding your core values:

>achievement: a sense of accomplishment or mastery

>advancement: promotions

>adventure: new and challenging experiences

>affection: love, caring

>competitiveness: winning, taking risks

>cooperation: working well with others, teamwork

creativity: being imaginative, innovative

economic security: having enough money to pay the bills

family happiness: a sense of well-being to you and your children and mate

freedom: independence, autonomy, choices

friendship: close relationships with others

health: being physically well and active

helpfulness: assisting others, improving society

immortality: everlasting fame

inner harmony: being at peace with yourself

integrity: honesty, standing up for your beliefs

involvement: participating with others, belonging

loyalty: duty, obedience

order: tranquility, stability, conformity

personal development: use of potential

pleasure: fun, laughs, a life with time for fun

power: control, authority or influence over others

recognition: respect from others, status

religion: strong beliefs in God, practicing your faith

responsibility: accountable for results

self-respect: pride, sense of personal identity

wealth: making money, getting rich

wisdom: understanding life, discovering knowledge

STEP TWO FOR ACHIEVING

The next step is equally simple. Once you've decided what you want, then you figure out what you want to do to live that value: these are your goals.

If you decide you want to be rich, how are you going to make that money? Working for someone, or starting your own business? Do you have the necessary education, job experience, and resources to accomplish that objective? Figure out whatever you need to do to get whatever it is you want. Those are your goals.

STEP THREE FOR ACHIEVING

Then quite simply, go to it. But not before you've written down your core values and goals. It is absolutely essential that you write these things down, in a special notebook, on a piece of paper that you keep in your desk or attached to a bulletin board, whatever, but write them down.

Writing values and goals down gives them great power because they then become concrete. You can read the words. Concrete ideas are more powerful that abstract ideas. By writing them down, they become concrete rather than thoughts in your head.

As is true in other areas of life, you only get what you ask for. When you write values and goals down, you are asking yourself to give yourself these things. This does something to your subconscious as well, giving the goals power in your mind.

Because they are written down, they are also measurable and you can assess your progress against them. You will make progress if you do the things I have said, and that progress will make you feel good, satisfied, and give you the momentum to keep going. Nothing succeeds like success. When you see your success, you will strive for further success because you will feel so good about your accomplishments.

When you write goals down, they also guide you in the many decisions you will make on the use of your time. There is too much to do in life. We need priorities to guide us on what we want to be doing. The fundamental choices you have made, your core values will also help determine your priorities. If raising happy confident children is important, maybe you'll forego an activity that is purely for your pleasure, and pick a family activity instead. If using your creative potential is a primary value, maybe you'd choose to go to school rather than be a volunteer in the community.

I set my goals once a year and do a major review every couple of years. Once I had decided to write a book on recovery from domestic abuse, my goal was very achievable, to write two pages a week. Although I sometimes wrote ten pages, and the next week wrote nothing, I achieved consistent progress throughout the year. When I finished, I had actually exceeded my goal by thirty pages.

NIBBLING AWAY AT YOUR GOALS

When you are advancing on your goals, keep in mind that the Swiss cheese effect works. You can nibble away at your goals; they don't have to be accomplished in one fell swoop. Maybe a core value is a nice home environment. Right now, your house might need major work to be your dream home. There are many intermediate measures you can take to make it livable, cosy, your personal environment. Maybe you need to paint it, that doesn't cost a lot of money, and use throw rugs until you can afford that new wall-to-wall carpeting or redo your wood floors.

I wrote the manuscript for this book in short time segments: an hour here and there, an occasional all day session when my children were gone. I could see the progress by looking back, and see the goal, by looking ahead, and I never felt frustrated or overwhelmed by the work. I just did the piece in front of me. Of course, I gave up some things other people would resent. I watch only a little television, my home is a little dirtier than it used to be, and I don't entertain the way I used to. But I so much enjoy the activity of writing that these changes were not tradeoffs. Sacrificing is giving up something you really want to do. If I really didn't want to write, then I didn't. I discovered that I usually chose to do so when I had the opportunity because it was so much fun.

I learned that patience does pay off and it is easier to be patient if you really want to get to the end goal.

ACHIEVING GOALS SHOULD GIVE SATISFACTION

Goals are important because achieving them gives us satisfaction. In the process of setting and achieving goals, don't forget that the process of achieving goals is our life. Everything we do should be pleasurable to us at some level and we should enjoy the process. Working to achieve goals is part of the secret; enjoying the process of achieving goals is the other part of the secret.

There is a parable by Robert J. Hastings, called "The Station", which captures this concept. I'd like to share it with you:

> Tucked away in our subconscious is an idyllic vision. We see ourselves on a long trip that spans the continent. We are traveling by train. Out the windows we drink in the passing scene of cars on nearby

highways, of children waving at a crossing, of cattle grazing on a distant hillside, of smoke pouring from a power plant, of row upon row of corn and wheat, of flatlands and valleys, of mountains and rolling hillsides, of city skylines and village halls.

But uppermost in our minds is the final destination. On a certain day at a certain hour we will pull into the station. Bands will be playing and flags waving. Once we get there so many wonderful dreams will come true and the pieces of our lives will fit together like a completed jigsaw puzzle. How restlessly we pace the aisles, damning the minutes for loitering -- waiting, waiting, waiting for the station.

"When we reach the station, that will be it!" we cry. "When I'm 18." "When I buy a new 450 SL Mercedes Benz!" "When I put the last kid through college." "When I have paid off the mortgage!" "When I get a promotion." "When I reach the age of retirement, I shall live happily every after!"

Sooner or later, we must realize there is no station, no one place to arrive at once and for all. The true joy of life is the trip. The station is only a dream. It constantly outdistances us."

"Relish the moment" is a good motto, especially when coupled with Psalm 118:24: "This is the day which the Lord hath made: we will rejoice and be glad in it." It isn't the burdens of today that drive men mad. It is the regrets over yesterday and the fear of tomorrow. Regret and fear are twin thieves who rob us of today.

So stop pacing the aisles and counting the miles. Instead, climb more mountains, eat more ice cream, go barefoot more often, swim more rivers, watch more sunsets, laugh more, cry less. Life must be lived as we go along. The station will come soon enough.

Samuel Johnson also said it, but shorter, "The process is the reality." As you strive for your goals, enjoy, savor, appreciate your life as much as possible. Focus on the now, the today, and all your tomorrows will take care of themselves.

How I define success hasn't changed much over the course of my recovery. What has changed is that by my standards, I am successful and that has given me great satisfaction.

As Fritz says in his book:

> The more you realize that what you truly want really matters the more selective you become about what you want. You recognize the importance of your deepest wants and less important ones take a secondary place.
> As you reunite with your power to create, most likely you will discover that what truly matters to you is worthy of you -- for example, health, freedom, justice, and being true to yourself.

Setting and achieving goals will make you feel worthy of your humanity and help you overcome any previously perceived shortcomings. It is so simple, yet so few take the time or make the effort to do it. By doing it for yourself, you will experience satisfaction; you will contribute your creative power to the world; and you will overcome the negative messages you used to believe about yourself. The old saying, "Nothing succeeds like success," is accurate. Once you experience the personal power that comes from achieving your dreams, you will not want to go back to living any other way. You will feel successful. You will be successful. You are doing what you want to do.

RECOMMENDATIONS FOR FURTHER WORK

1. Write down your core values. Use the list in the chapter to help decide what they are. Go through and pick ten values on your first pass. Go back and narrow it down to five. Write those down. Then write down your goals based on the values. Make a short, medium, and long range plan. Short-term is what you want to accomplish between now and a year. Medium is from 1-3 years. Long-range is 3 -5 years.

2. Don't be afraid to revise your list. It's your list. As you get into the process, you'll catch the spirit.

3. Take time to dream. Dream your dreams. Then figure out how you'll reach them.

CHAPTER EIGHT

YOU CAN BUILD HEALTHY RELATIONSHIPS

    I have gone through all the stages any divorced person goes through in regards to re-establishing intimate relationships with men. In the first stage, I declared emphatically and believed completely that I would never marry or date again. I think that this stage is understandable and healthy. Rushing headlong into another relationship after leaving one that didn't work is a bad idea. You have to end the relationship mentally and emotionally and grieve for its passing. You have to heal and work on yourself before you can consider getting involved in a healthy relationship.
    I have watched all sorts of women move from one dysfunctional relationship into another. Maybe they're addicted to being in love. If that is the case, the rush of a fresh romance temporarily masks their feelings about themselves and they can escape their feeling of being inadequate. But once the bloom of the romance wears off, they find themselves back to reality, trying to interact and develop intimacy and they don't know how or they're

involved with someone who doesn't know how. These women may not like themselves so they can hardly let themselves be intimate for to do so would expose the self they don't like.

By telling myself I wasn't going to get involved with a man again, I gave myself plenty of time to recover. As I healed and moved into my new life, I began to realize how lonely I was for male companionship. I was plenty busy. My two daughters, my job, my volunteer activities, and my home gave me much to do, but I missed the companionship of a man. I had many women friends and a few men friends but what I felt a yearning for was a close and intimate relationship with the opposite sex.

I then entered the next stage, one of tentatively re-establishing relationships with men, albeit somewhat superficial. I tried some low-key experimental dating. I say tentatively because at that point I wasn't sure if I wanted to begin any involvement with men that might lead to intimacy. Although the dating was low-key, the effect on me was highly stressful. I became so nervous before a date, even a non-threatening one (in reality, they were all threatening), that I developed diarrhea, stomach aches and headaches. I would shake visibly and was certain my dates could tell how nervous I was. (They probably could!) I had a difficult time relaxing during the date, acting naturally, and enjoying myself. During this stage, even the slightest resemblance to my ex-husbands caused me to end the relationship before it began. Something relatively minor like a tone of voice or an action could cause me to be sure I was making a mistake.

Then quite subtly I hit the stage of being able to relax and enjoy dating. I'm sure the fact that I felt more certain of who I was, that I liked myself and felt self-assured and confident had something to do with my enjoyment. Because of my confidence, I was also able to say "no thanks" to men whom I found not to my liking for whatever reason without feeling anxiety or pain. I was pretty certain by the third date whether I wanted to continue seeing the man or not. I was fortunate in dating a lot of men who enjoyed me, and their compliments about my looks, my hair, my jokes, my dancing added to my confidence and made me feel desirable to men. This boosted my confidence as well but also made me feel that I didn't have to accept the first warm body that came my way. I could be picky about with whom I got involved.

I made it a point to date a variety of men, not just businessmen but laborers, artists, social workers, etc. I found that I usually learned something from each of them and found a different kind of enjoyment with each one.

The final stage is to find a mutually satisfying relationship with a man and deepen it into a commitment of some form. I haven't reached that stage yet, maybe I never will, but I have observed some friends that have. I recently attended a wedding of a friend who had been single 13 years after her divorce. She married a wonderful man and I have no doubt that they will be happy. They dated four or five years before they committed to marriage. I have several other divorced friends that waited five to nine years to find someone they were compatible with and they now have happy long-term marriages. Another friend had been married three times, all losers, but is now married to a stable, loving, kind man and is very contented and happy. I also have friends who have chosen to not remarry and they tell me that they, too, are happy. Some of these are involved with men in long term commitments but have chosen not to marry. Others are involved but not long term and others are simply not interested. The variety of life styles available to women today is endless. I believe anything is now possible. We do not have to be part of a couple to be happy fulfilled people.

WHY SELF-ESTEEM IS SO IMPORTANT IN RELATIONSHIPS

To build a long term, stable and trusting relationship, a woman must first of all like herself. There are many traps that will occur in a relationship between a man and a woman if the woman or man does not have positive self-esteem. A person who has positive self-esteem believes that happiness is their birthright and is self-directing in obtaining that happiness. If you do not have positive self-esteem, you will experience constant anxiety over the happiness you feel from your relationship and that anxiety will create trouble for you. The way that anxiety will be displayed will be varied. It may be the need for constant reassurance that you are loved. You may demand to hear it or have it displayed constantly.

The anxiety may come up when you compare yourself unfavorably to other women, either privately or with your partner, and then wait anxiously for affirmation that you are better than the other women. Your uncertainty that you have the right to happiness may be exhibited as jealousness and possessiveness, which a women who has low self-esteem may not be able to control even though she knows it is senseless and self-defeating. The woman may also watch herself behave in a mean manner so that she can test her partner's devotion to her over and over.

A woman with low self-esteem may also find herself using manipulation and control techniques so that she can maintain the relationship artificially because she does not believe it can exist any other way. She may tell her man that his love for her is not deserved, and may say it over and over, always aware of the danger of saying this, but doing it over and over.

The woman who has low self-esteem may criticize and belittle this man who is trying to please her. In doing so, she is trying to exert power over him because she does not believe she is worthy and by picking on him, reduces him to her level.

What all these behaviors add up to is that she simply cannot accept love. She cannot believe she is lovable so she tries to be unlovable or destroy that love because she doesn't believe happiness is possible. Instead of giving in to the happiness and going with it, she creates a miserable situation for both of them, and thereby drives him away, or if he is not driven away, kills the intimacy so that love can not bloom. Either way, she has proven her point that she does not deserve happiness and she is not happy, which makes her relieved, but she still is not happy.

I understand all these behaviors from the point of view of being in a relationship with someone who exhibited them. I believe men who abuse have low self-esteem and they cannot accept love or give love because they do not believe they themselves are lovable.

In an earlier chapter, I talked about the importance of having good friendships. I want to state explicitly that you cannot expect to have an intimate relationship with a man if you do not know how to have an intimate friendship with anyone, man or woman. A romantic relationship is really based on friendship, which is the foundation that will exist once the passion has peaked and faded. No one in the history of the world has been able to keep passion alive indefinitely. No one has the energy. Exposure to someone for an extended period of time is bound to take the bloom off the rose. What committed partners have found is that the passion is replaced by stability, friendship, understanding, and sharing that far exceeds passion in its ability to withstand the ups and downs of life.

DEFINITION OF LOVE

Let us define what romantic love is. I like the definition that Nathaniel Branden uses in his book <u>The Psychology of Romantic Love.</u> That definition is "a passionate, spiritual-emotional-sexual attachment between a man and a woman that reflects a high regard for the value of each other's person." Ultimately romantic love is "to know and love his or her person."

When a person is romantically involved, there is a meeting of the total person, a temporary merging of two people into one, and then a melting back into two separate persons. That happens over and over but the important point is that the merging, although ecstasy, is always temporary, although the ability to repeat it over and over with the same person is what makes it special. The merging is mental, emotional, physical, spiritual, all or more occurring at the same time. Hopefully, the person we love, loves us for who we are and is eager to know who we are as fully as they can and we to show them our true selves.

To build a stable, trusting relationship, a woman must "Go slow." If you meet someone you like, don't feel like you've met a human red light special available for only ten minutes. You do not have to throw caution to the wind and bare your soul, lower your boundaries, and risk losing everything you've been working to gain. Give yourself plenty of time to get better acquainted. If he's that wonderful, he, too, will want to go slowly in establishing a relationship.

How much trust and how soon is a critical point. If you trust too soon or fail to exercise caution, you may not allow yourself to really know the man well enough to be sure you're not making a mistake. If you hold trust back and don't allow the man to know your true self, you may put up roadblocks to establishing intimacy. Somewhere in between is the balance point which you and he must find.

For starters, be neutral about the man. Do not automatically assume he is some kind of god. Do not romanticize him and create a beautiful history with him after only a few hours of his company. Some of us are very good about fantasizing and can create a beautiful future which is based only on our expectations and desires and needs and not on the reality of his personality, character and soul.

On the other hand, don't assume the opposite, that some guy is a zero because he doesn't look the way you think he should or would like him to look. I've concluded that some of the nicest husbands in the world are the balding paunchy one who wear white socks and old sweaters but treat their wives with love and kindness and have since they were married.

HOW TO MEET MEN

We need to also start from the assumption that you meet men. It is, all singles seem to agree, one of the most difficult things today, to meet someone who is interesting, unmarried, and interested in you. It can seem like the only ones out there are out there because they were rejected by someone else for good reason or they do not know how to build a relationship. But again, my eternal optimism pops up and I believe if you keep your eyes open, you might find someone meant for you. My one caution is that you should not invest in the proposition that without a man you are nothing. If you cannot find someone after searching, you still have an interesting life, believe in yourself, and have friends that love you for who you are, and that you are doing what you want to do.

Before you can meet anyone, you really have to be a friendly person. Be friendly; act friendly; look friendly. That ought to get you something right there. If nothing else, people will think you're simply a friendly person. You'll meet lots of folks, young, old, male, female, and probably learn a lot about the world and the people in it. You simply can't meet anyone if you walk around looking angry, shy, embarrassed, and self-conscious. If you can just forget about yourself, and focus on others, you'll meet tons of new friends. Shyness really comes from a form of shame, and if you've done your work on yourself, you won't be shy and you'll be receptive to the possibilities.

I also believe that people with positive feelings about themselves are more attractive physically. Their spirit shines through their physical characteristics and fills them with light, beauty and attraction. If you like yourself, you will carry your body with grace, meet others' eyes, and dazzle the world with a happy smile. All your physical imperfections will become unique aspects of you rather than detractors of physical beauty. The way to be beautiful is to feel beautiful.

I was terribly shy as a teenager. In fact, I joke and say I never saw anything but my two feet until I was 28 because I was so busy looking down at my feet and not at other people. Most people feel a little self-conscious when they meet someone for the first time, but now that I'm more confident, I realize how silly that really is. We take ourselves so seriously. We think we have to look a certain way, act a certain way, talk a certain way to be popular. If we could just understand that if we relaxed, enjoyed ourselves, and didn't try so hard to impress other people, we would have a wonderful time in life.

Another way you won't meet people is by staying home by yourself. You have to go out into the world to meet people. They are not going to come to you. The kinds of activities people engage in are endless. There are exercise and sports activities, plays and art shows, classes and workshops, volunteer activities of myriad assortment, dance classes and church activities to name a few. Better than just going to these things, get actively involved: hold an office, organize an event, volunteer to be more than just a member.

You can meet people through friends. It's amazing how often you meet a friend of a friend and then run into that new acquaintance within days of the meeting. Here your paths had crossed and you didn't even know it. You yourself can throw parties and invite people you want to get to know better. They can be big fancy parties, small dinner parties, casual potlucks, surprise birthday parties, holiday parties, backyard barbecues. The variety is endless.

You can meet people while you're pursuing an interest, such as attending an auction, browsing at an antique or stamp or garden show. You can start a club for your interest: book, food, singles, cards, whatever.

One of the modern ways to meet the opposite sex is through the personals ads in the papers. I have friends who have friends, or so they say, that met their mate through personals ads. Although I would recommend placing rather than answering, you will have a good time meeting all these people who took the time to write you a letter, and who knows, one of them might be the one.

You can meet men while travelling. Today there are vacation spots and vacation clubs that cater to singles. You could take a singles cruise or join a singles club that organizes events and social activities for the unattached. Even if you don't meet the one for you, you will meet other people and see some sights and do interesting things at the same time.

HOW TO MEASURE SOMEONE YOU MEET

Let's say you do meet someone following these suggestions. Try to influence your activity choices so that they are fun, non-threatening, and allow for as much interaction between the two of you as possible. Going to a movie is probably the worst date two people who don't know each other very well could pick. You can't talk; you sit side by side feeling uncomfortable and you don't get to see a range of reactions. What happens when the guy loses at bowling? Does he have good table manners? Can he hold up his end of the conversation at dinner? How does he act at a party: mingle well, or drink too much and become a boor to the other guests? When you have to wait in line, how does he handle it? What happens when you and he get lost on your way to something, does he handle it well or get upset and angry with you? All these behaviors give you clues to his personality and temperament.

I talk about how you need to have friends before you can build an intimate relationship. The same goes for your male dates. I would pay very close attention to their friendships. Do they have friends besides the people they work with? You are looking for indicators that they are healthy, whole people and having friends is an indicator. Someone who is healthy is pursuing interests, has a network of friends, is self-supporting and has a positive outlook on life. You do not need to get involved with someone who is a loser and is waiting to be rescued. You will regret it. You will become part of dysfunctionality again if you're not careful.

Other indicators that I consider important is if their behavior matches their words, even in little things, or perhaps especially in little things. I have very little patience for people who do not follow through on the things they promise. They are not dependable, trustworthy people. Even showing up at the proper time is an indicator of dependability. If they say they will call, and then fail to, and do that over and over, they are also indicating their unreliability.

If they say you are wonderful, and they love you so, yet don't ask what your wishes are, or honor your wishes, that is another important indicator in my mind of their mindset. They may regard themselves as the center of the world, and are indicating that to you so pay attention to the signals. When the excitement is gone, and the relationship is old, you will find out exactly where you stand, and it won't be where you want to be!

Even their manners, which are really courtesies of respect to others, display many clues of true character. A courteous man will hold the door, will hold your coat, will let you go first. I am a very modern, independent woman, yet in a romantic relationship, those courtesies tell me that he treasures me as a woman. I find it very distasteful to be treated second class, to be pushed aside while he goes first, walks out without waiting, and orders first. In my experience, the man who treats you well and displays good manners is the man who respects you for your independence too.

There is a tendency when you meet someone to tell them your life story. While you need to be honest, I don't think you have to lay out every detail of your life right away. I'm not saying to hide anything, but telling your life story may sound like a soap opera. I used to feel compelled to tell the whole story right away, and I am a completely honest person. But I began to see that the upfront approach could scare someone off. I may have been divorced twice, but I don't see myself as a loser or as a person who chose to have all these things happen. I know I am well liked by my acquaintances and respected by them as well. So I try and let that show through before I tell all. On the other hand, it's a fine line to walk. I dated a man who didn't tell me the whole story right away, which was fine with me, but he also merged a few important facts. He failed to mention that his son was not from a marriage but from a relationship that happened after a divorce and that the mother worked at the same office he did and he saw her everyday. He had legal custody of his son, and appeared to be a good father, but when I had them both come for a day of family type activities and eating, I noticed that he disciplined his son in a way that I didn't think was healthy. Those two things caused me to break off the relationship. I feel I wasted about six months on him.

I also went out once with a man who revealed his ex had a restraining order against him. Maybe she was crazy, as he said, but I thought it was a good idea not to get involved.

While you're building trust, rely on your gut reactions about the fellow. Sometimes we have unconscious reactions to a person that are so subtle we aren't aware of them. If your stomach gets a funny feeling or little alarms go off in your head when one story doesn't jive with a previous story, pay attention.It could save you a lot of grief later.

I dated a man that was older than I. He told me he was 12 years older, but frankly he looked 22 years older. He was exciting, and fun, and I enjoyed his company. He treated me right and was crazy about me. But as we got into talking about our lives, I started adding up the number of years he worked here, lived there, and I came up with the conclusion that the feeling I had that he was whacking a decade off his age was correct. Furthermore, he was more than willing to show me that he had been tested for AIDS, but unwilling to show me his driver's license. I said good bye to him, with a little regret, but certainly didn't want involvement with someone who wasn't truthful.

I also think trust building is a little like playing ball. You toss it; he tosses it back. You show a little more of yourself; he reveals a little more too. You show a little vulnerability; he shows a little. You suggest an activity; he suggest an activity. It's not scorekeeping, but it is paying attention to who is doing all the work in the relationship. You can't build a relationship all by yourself; you need involvement from the other party. In my experience, men seem very weak in the area of throwing the ball back. They would just like to lean back and go along for the ride. I dated a very nice man for a while. With him, I really worked to keep the relationship moving. I finally had to wake up to the fact that he either didn't want to or didn't know how to build a long-term commitment. Initially I decided to break it off. I did find that I missed him a great deal and re-established the relationship as a friend. I don't think he realizes what I went through, that I was in pain, and that I chose to just be friends, because of his lack of desire for intimacy. But the decision freed me to look past him and meet others. Although I may always like him a great deal, my expectations are minimal with him because I have no desire to do all the work in a relationship .

The biggest change for me is that I do not define myself as belonging to someone else. I have learned how to have fun and enjoy life alone, with my children, with friends, and with a man. I have invested energy in fulfilling a happiness prophecy for myself. No matter what happens, I have a solid foundation for my life. On the other hand, I haven't completely shut myself off from possibilities.

In drug and alcohol recovery, there is a belief that we must "let go and let God," meaning we sometimes think but we actually don't make everything happen in our life or control everything in our life. Trusting that my life is going to go the way it should so that I will be happy has helped me relax and be open but not needy for male relationships. The health of my emotional and psychological life helps me keep balance and understand that the lack of a committed relationship does not mean I cannot be a happy, fulfilled person. I am happy and fulfilled just as I am. What I am looking for is even more happiness, even more fulfillment. That is the standard by which I measure potential relationships: if they will add more, not take away from, my happiness.

RECOMMENDATIONS FOR FURTHER WORK

1. If you do not have any fun activities for yourself, find some. Make a list of all the possible clubs, classes, or groups you could get involved in, and pick one of them. Make it your focus and do more than just be a passive member. Reach out through involvement.

2. Set a goal to do some entertaining in your home in your own style. Select the guests carefully, and plan the menu and then organize the event so that you can fully enjoy yourself.

3. If you are invited to something, go! Feeling depressed and lacking energy are fed by aloneness. Take advantage of every opportunity presented to you to have fun.

Chapter Nine

You Are On The Path

I would be lying to you if I said you will heal so completely that it will be as if the abuse never happened. It happened and left scars. All scars were once wounds. The wound is filled in, but it is still there. You are the way you are today because of your experiences. Your experiences do not have to be excuses for not being happy. Your experiences do not have to limit you in reaching out for all that life has to offer and you to offer it. Your experiences have tested you and you have become strong.

I have a large scar on my right thigh. When I was three years old, I found and played with a book of matches. The flame set my sun suit on fire and caused a third degree burn on my leg. The scar has healed and even diminished over the years. Most of the time I don't even see it; the scar is so much a part of my body. I am aware of it when a stranger may see it when I go swimming, or undress in front of someone I don't know well.

The abuse you experienced is the same thing. It has healed for me, and it will heal for you. The pain has been covered over with scar tissue. As you go about your life, the abuse will begin to fade and you will go hours, days, or weeks without thinking about it. However, there will be triggering incidents for you when you will recall the abuse. Sometimes when I am discouraged, hurt, or tired, and I yearn to be nurtured and loved by someone, but cannot ask for what I need, I feel the scars from the abuse. Sometimes when I am disappointed by someone who did not keep their word, I feel the scars. Sometimes when I feel shamed by an experience that for others would not be an experience of shame, I feel the scars. Your triggering incidents will be unique to your experience of abuse. Over time, the intensity of your reaction to the triggering incidents will diminish and you will develop creative and nurturing ways to handle them.

Mother's Day is a problem for me. That was the day I was scared for my life. Mother's Day creates flashbacks for me, memories of abuse and isolation. I become depressed, feel unloved, unworthy, and am unable to control my emotions. I've had thirteen Mother's Days occur since the actual event, and by now I am wise to how my emotions will go on that day. I have been able to compress the experience into a short period of time whereas initially I felt depressed and unworthy and unloved for weeks. It is a day that I know will be difficult and I remind myself of that early on. I remind myself how far I've come, how well I have it, how loved I am, and all those things help. I remain hopeful that the memories will continue to diminish over time and I will be able to enjoy the day fully. My daughters' loving gifts help; their concern for a mother who so rarely cries uncontrollably but does it on a day meant to honor her touches me. I understand also that fathers do a lot to make their children understand the significance of the day and as a single parent I miss some of that support. My second daughter's father does a good job helping my youngest remember me on all the special occasions of the year, but my first has kept true to form since the beginning.

Silence between myself and another person also used to be a triggering incident for shame. My second ex-husband often would not talk to me for days, and when I am with someone who does not talk I feel some of the old anxiety coming back. Simply recognizing that as an experience that had a lot of bad feelings for me helped me learn that I did not have to interpret the silence that way.

I would like to never have experienced abuse. But I cannot go back. You cannot go back. We are what we are because of our experiences. So you have a choice. You can choose to stay stuck in the pain and unhappiness or you can go forward with your wounds and heal them. You can go on living with scars and find that not only is life salvageable; it is wonderful.

I can remember sitting at my kitchen table and weeping. I was sure that I would never find happiness. I believed that my life was over and I felt such overwhelming self-pity and hate and pain that I wanted it to be over right then and there. But I had to go on. I stopped crying, wiped my tears, and set up the coffee pot for the morning and went to bed hoping tomorrow would be a better day. Each day I did that until one day I woke up and realized tomorrow was here, and life was better. Slowly, gradually, the scar tissue formed and I was able to heal and carry on with the important business of living.

ABUSE SETS YOU APART

Today I am happy, but I still feel my scars and occasionally pity myself and wish that I had been dealt a different hand of cards. I am aware that abuse has set me apart from other women who have not known that kind of rejection and hate. I am more fragile in my feelings and expectations. I know complete disappointment as a result of being hurt by someone I loved. If I sometimes expect so little today, it is because I received so little then. If I am sometimes so unsure of my feelings today, it is because I was told how wrong they were then. If I sometimes suffer silently today, it is because for so long I had no one to share my heartfelt feelings with to lighten the load.

I also know that there is no such thing as perfection. Life is imperfect; people are imperfect; there are always problems. It is not the absence of problems that is the key to happiness; it is how we deal with them. When I feel my scars, I remember that I do know how to resolve problems and cope with situations that are not good. I remember and I feel better and I regain my cheerfulness and optimism.

You too have something special that sets you apart. The scars on your heart have taught you to deal with the problems of life. Because a scar has two sides-- the ugly side, the price of pain, loneliness and despair-- and the beautiful side -- the courage, strength and patience it took to face your problems and deal with them.

YOU HAVE COURAGE

Abuse happens every sixteen seconds in this country. Not every woman leaves and makes a better life. Many, many women stay to live out their years in pain, fear, despair. You didn't choose that path. You had the courage to leave while you could still do so. You had the courage to fight back. You had the courage to listen to your heart and know there was a better life for you.

That courage will stand you well in life. You are a special person because of your courage. You should applaud yourself and realize how brave and wonderful you are. In the face of all that courage, your scars aren't going to hold you back from grabbing what life has to offer and daring to be yourself.

Your scars represent your ability to rise above and resolve problems. No one is asking you to be perfect and you can approach your life with charity towards yourself. Charity and self-acceptance are different from excuse making. Charity and self-acceptance create awareness that you have some barriers to work through, not to use them as stop signs. Charity and self-acceptance will help you get closer to the warmth of self-love. Self-love will create a desire in you to recognize what your issues are and to deal with those issues. You don't have to work through them all at once. Slowly and patiently, you can direct your life in the direction you want it to go. You will be better for constantly believing that you are acting, doing, and being just as you should be for this stage in your recovery. You will unfold and become more and more whole as time passes. You will get sudden insights, and slow realizations of how you want to become and you will go in that direction. Always you will be growing, becoming, and staying alive and well emotionally and psychologically.

WHAT HAPPENS WHEN LIFE IS NORMAL

You will get to the point where a "normal" life style will be your life. You will lose your fear that someone close to you is going to get upset and angry and blame and abuse you. You will gradually become spontaneous without the need to guard yourself so carefully and consider every action. When you get to that point, you will discover that problems still exist. Your sense of what is normal will change and in your new normal life, you will also have problems. You will still get depressed, and there are times when you will be hurt, angry, or discouraged. You will need to remember all the steps you have taken in the past to work out of those feelings. You will have to feel your feelings, choose how to act on them, set priorities, affirm yourself, locate your values on this issue and move on to a solution with faith that taking care of the present is the best insurance for a good future.

Sometimes it will be instantaneous. You'll encounter a small obstacle and without much effort, deal with it and move on. Other times, you will get all mucked up in feelings of martyrdom, of being stuck and you may chase those feelings around for weeks or months until you find out what is wrong and how to fix it. Sometimes it will be easy. Other times it will be hard and take a long time. And occasionally it will be beyond your power and you'll have to accept the situation and change your attitude.

In life, the pendulum keeps on swinging back and forth and while nothing good lasts forever neither does the bad. Everything will pass or you'll get the strength and courage to deal with it. We live in a state of constant flux and must always be dealing with a changing present reality. But if we are sure of our values, if we live with love for ourselves and others, believe in our ability to deal with today, we can overcome even the worst of these experiences. Unless you choose to become involved again in a dysfunctional relationship, you are going to be happy the rest of your life, which is not the same as being trouble-free. Everyone has problems and troubles. You will too. The idea that happiness can continue on indefinitely is alien, even frightening to you. You may even feel great anxiety about being happy. In time, you will realize that you can be happy. You can feel relaxed and let go. No longer will you need to be in constant control of everything that happens.

When you were abused, you tried to control the abuse from happening. You now know that we each choose how to act on our feelings and that your efforts to control the abuser were impossible attempts. You need to give up that pattern of control. You can only control your own actions. There is a larger natural flow to life. Look around the world of nature and observe the flow of night into day, of fall into winter and winter into spring. The birds follow their instincts and fly south in winter.

There is a tempo and pace to the world that people do not cause nor affect. Have faith that the higher power who created and directed our beautiful world created a tempo and flow to your life as well. We cannot make everything happen. Some of it happens naturally and if we could just relax and give in to it, we too would find an ebb and flow to our life that suits us perfectly. If you can be yourself, the power of your spirit would create a ripple in the world outside your control. You don't have to force it, make it happen, or cause it. Your natural energy will be guided by a higher power. We must trust this to happen and feel free to be ourselves.

LETTING GO OF HATE

You know that you are lovable and deserve to be loved. As part of your recovery, you have learned to love yourself. By loving yourself, you are able to love others. You can trust yourself to love. Because I loved myself, I was able to release my hatred towards my ex-husbands. I understand at some level that they did not intend to be abusive any more than I intended to be abused. They lacked something inside themselves and they were emotionally ill. I pity them. I hope that they are healing too. Although I will never be friendly with them or like them, I do not hate them. Hate is like cancer. It grows and multiplies and consumes the health and life within us. To heal completely, you have to let your hate go. By letting my hate go, thoughts of them are only concerned with the present, such as their relationship with my daughters or whether or not I've received my monthly support payments. I used to dwell on the past. I used to want them dead. Those thoughts and wishes weren't good for me. They kept me stuck in the past and I wanted to move out of the past. I may not respect them. I may feel irritated by them but I don't hate them. For me, letting my hate go involved sending it off in a mental balloon and watching the balloon go "poof" in the breeze. I felt freer and lighter after I did that.

CHANGING YOUR RELATIONSHIP WITH A FORMER PARTNER

I still had to teach them that they don't control me. It's amazing to look back and realize that although we divorced, they still assumed that our relationship was based on the same patterns. Their expectation was they could tell me what to do. Their expectation was that they could belittle me when I did not do it their way. They assumed I would not have needs of my own and they assumed that they could create the rules. I needed to teach them how to interact with me and that our relationship was changed. I was changed and I was not accepting a relationship with them with the old rules still intact. I truly wasn't recovered until I did that. I tried to avoid doing that for some time, hoping that by avoiding them, I could avoid the issue.

When I confronted the issue that I could teach others how I wanted to be treated, what I learned was that it changed me. There were no more bogy men in my closet. The worst thing that could happen is that they got angry. They yelled on the phone. They demanded and threatened. But they didn't hurt me and they calmed down and I got what I wanted or a compromise was reached between the two of us. I was afraid when I did it. I took one to court to make my point that our divorce judgment had obligations on both sides. It cost me almost as much to take him to court as it did for the medical bills he was supposed to pay. But it was the principle of the thing and I wanted to make sure he was educated on what that principle was. I wanted him to know that he couldn't push me around anymore. It changed me because I learned that I had become the kind of person who stood up for herself. You have to do it over and over before you can feel confident that you are different and this new self-assertion isn't a temporary aberration. You can and want to be treated with respect.

DARE TO BE YOURSELF

Then I realized that this new attitude would allow me to dare to be myself. For the first time in years, I felt in control of my life. I could do what I wanted, be self-directing. I wasn't just surviving, just protecting, I was striving to be who I am.

Integration of your new attitudes and beliefs and translating them consistently into action takes time. But once you truly love yourself everything else falls into place. Your choices become healthy. Your choices become healthy in all areas: work, life style, relationships, and values. What is truly meaningful and worthwhile becomes different.

What I treasure in my life most today are the simple and fundamental things. I have two daughters who are my biggest treasure. Our family unit is healthy and happy. I enjoy raising them, despite the hard work, and relating to them. I enjoy working, knowing that it represents my self-sufficiency. Work gives me a place to go contribute what I can. I enjoy my home, humble though it be, and entering it after being gone and knowing it to be a safe and comfortable haven that I have provided. I treasure my flower beds because they offer me an opportunity to create a spot of beauty for myself and others. I treasure my cats, meowing constantly for food because I am important to them. I treasure my friends who call me when I am too busy to call them or sense some unhappiness and let me know it matters to them how I feel. I treasure my relatives, who have shared their lives with me. I treasure nature and its beauty and generosity. The list goes on and on. None of them cost much if anything, none of them can't be found by anyone else. These gifts are all out there waiting for you to find them for yourself.

All the people and things I treasure, all the things I do that I truly like are in one way or another connected to love. I know these treasures would not have the same meaning if I did not have so much unhappiness in my past. The petty things in life are not worth wasting time on. I watch others and see some who do not really see what they have. I see others who learned their lesson about what is a treasure in life in other ways than mine, but in ways that have meant pain in some form or another. None of us escape pain. Some of us learn from it and use it to our advantage to make the best of what is left.

LIVE WITH YOUR WHOLE HEART

You have to live with your whole heart. Halfheartedly you just don't enjoy it, appreciate it, or savor it if you're not in there with your sleeves rolled up, sweating and working and playing and laughing. If you hold back, thinking that is the safe way, the sure way, what you get is half a life. Maybe you're avoiding some risks that way and that might mean avoiding some pain, but you're also cheating yourself by thinking that you're experiencing what life has to offer. Life offers it all, bad, good, happiness, sadness, thrills, disappointments, hate, love, anxiety, calmness, coldness, and warmth. You take it all and you make the best that you can with it.

You are on the path to happiness. It may not be an even and smooth path, but it's heading in the right direction. Trust love, love of self and love for others, and you will find your treasures here on earth.

BIBLIOGRAPHY

Beattie, Melody. Beyond Codependency and getting better all the time. New York City, New York: Harper & Row, Publishers, Inc., 1989.

Beattie, Melody. Codependent No More. New York City, New York: Harper & Row, Publishers, Inc., 1987.

Branden, Nathaniel. The Psychology of Romantic Love. New York City, New York: Bantam Books, 1981.

Bradshaw, John. Healing The Shame That Binds You. Deerfield Beach, Florida: Health Communications, Inc., 1988.

Forward, Dr. Susan and Joan Torres. Men Who Hate Women & The Women Who Love Them. New York City, New York: Bantam Books, 1986.

Fossum, Merle A. and Marilyn J. Mason. Facing Shame: Families in Recovery. New York City, New York: W.W. Norton & Company, 1986.

Fritz, Robert M. The Path of Least Resistance: Principles for Creating What You Want to Create. Walpole, New Hampshire: Stillpoint Press, 1986.

Kaufman, Gershen with Lev Raphael. The Dynamics of Power: Building A Competent Self. Cambridge, Massachusetts: Schenkman Books, Inc., 1983.

Merwin, Sandra J. Real Self: The Inner Journey of Courage. Minnetonka, Minnesota: TigerLily Press, 1991.

Myers, Isabel Briggs with Peter B. Myers. <u>Gifts Differing</u>. Palo Alto, California: Consulting Psychologists Press, Inc., 1980.

Walker, Lenore E. <u>The Battered Woman</u>. New York City, New York: Harper & Row, 1979.

About the Author

Candace Hennekens is communications manager for a computer manufacturer. She has worked in employee communications, public relations, training and development, human resources management, and real estate. She has a Bachelors Degree in Journalism from Northwestern University, Evanston, Illinois, and a Masters Degree in Management Science from Cardinal Stritch College, Milwaukee, Wisconsin.

She has two daughters and lives in the Midwest in a small town. She has served on volunteer boards for various organizations, including the Salvation Army, Displaced Homemakers Project, and the University of Wisconsin-Eau Claire Business Extension. She is certified as a Myers Briggs consultant. She is active in school and church activities.

Ms. Hennekens is the founder and owner of ProWriting Services and Press. Her company's mission is to publish self-help materials for women of all ages to make their lives better. "My greatest accomplishment," she says, "is healing the damage from domestic violence and becoming a whole person again. I did it for myself because I believe that life has much to offer those who seek out the best that it offers. I want to be a positive role model for two of the most important people in my life, my daughters."

Order Form for Additional Copies of this Book

Cut out box and mail to:

ProWriting Services and Press
415 Terrill Street
Chippewa Falls, Wisconsin 54729
715/723-8799

Write for information about quantity discounts.

One copy costs $6.95 plus $2.00 shipping and handling. Wisconsin Residents please add 35 cents for 5% sales tax. Chippewa County Residents please add 38 cents for 5.5% sales tax.

Thank you for your order!

Please send me __ copies of <u>Healing Your Life: Recovery from Domestic Abuse</u>.

Enclosed is my check or money order for _____ ($6.95 per book plus $2.00 postage and handling plus sales tax if applicable.) Book will be sent first class mail or UPS.

Name_____

Address_____

City_____

State_____

Zip Code_____